PARLOUR GAMES FOR MODERN FAMILIES

MYFANWY JONES
& SPIRI TSINTZIRAS

PENGUIN BOOKS

PENGUIN BOOKS

Published by the Penguin Group
Penguin Books Ltd, 80 Strand, London WC2R 0RL, England
Penguin Group (USA) Inc., 375 Hudson Street, New York, New York 10014, USA
Penguin Group (Canada), 90 Eglinton Avenue East, Suite 700, Toronto, Ontario, Canada M4P 2Y3
(a division of Pearson Penguin Canada Inc.)
Penguin Ireland, 25 St Stephen's Green, Dublin 2, Ireland (a division of Penguin Books Ltd)
Penguin Group (Australia), 250 Camberwell Road, Camberwell, Victoria 3124, Australia
(a division of Pearson Australia Group Pty Ltd)
Penguin Books India Pvt Ltd, 11 Community Centre, Panchsheel Park,
New Delhi – 110 017, India
Penguin Group (NZ), 67 Apollo Drive, Rosedale, North Shore 0632, New Zealand
(a division of Pearson New Zealand Ltd)
Penguin Books (South Africa) (Pty) Ltd, 24 Sturdee Avenue,
Rosebank, Johannesburg 2196, South Africa

Penguin Books Ltd, Registered Offices: 80 Strand, London WC2R 0RL, England

www.penguin.com

First published in Australia by Scribe Publications 2009
Published in Penguin Books 2010

010

Copyright © Myfanwy Jones & Spiri Tsintziras, 2009
All rights reserved

The moral rights of the authors have been asserted

Printed in Great Britain by Clays Ltd, St Ives plc

ISBN: 978-1-846-14347-2

www.greenpenguin.co.uk

MIX
Paper from
responsible sources
FSC
www.fsc.org
FSC™ C018179

Penguin Books is committed to a sustainable
future for our business, our readers and our planet.
This book is made from Forest Stewardship
Council™ certified paper.

ALWAYS LEARNING   **PEARSON**

CONTENTS

WORDS BIG AND SMALL, LONG AND TALL

INTRODUCTION
THE CASE FOR GAMES

In the true man there is a child concealed who wants to play.
— Friedrich Nietzsche

We were sitting in the park, two mothers, watching our children play and reminiscing about childhood games. Wink Murder, Consequences, Dictionary, Cheat … we hadn't thought about these games in years. They were fantastic, we reminded one another. Our children would love them! And they didn't involve screens, or require a trip to Kmart. Why didn't we play more?

We noticed that even talking about games made us feel good, made us smile.

We managed to recall a handful of games, but decades of information overload — of red wine and caffeine and deadlines and babies and odd socks and hastily scribbled lists and news updates and crashing computers and rushing and still being late — meant that most had left the memory bank, or had disintegrated beyond recognition.

We needed a book to turn to, a record of all the games in solid print. And so it was that *Parlour Games for Modern Families* became a twinkle in our eyes, and then a publishing proposal and, finally, many games — and a great many laughs — later, here it is with all its fingers and toes. We wanted it for our own use, and figured there would be other families who would want it, too. This simple motive has guided us all the way through.

But what are parlour games, why do we think they're so great, and what can you expect from this book?

THE GOLDEN AGE OF PARLOUR GAMES

A parlour is just a living room, and parlour games are group games played in said room. Easy. In historical terms, however, 'parlour games' generally refer to those diversions enjoyed in British and American — and, to a lesser extent, Australian — parlours of the Victorian era. In the wake of the Industrial Revolution, well-to-do families had more leisure time than their predecessors, and this gave rise to a whole new generation of games involving wordplay, memory, logic, dramatic skills, and acts of absurd and pointless fun. These games were often played at small evening parties with family and friends; think *Mansfield Park* and the gay goings-on in the parlour after supper.

Most Victorian parlour games used equipment found in the home, and tended to be imaginative, resourceful, and overwhelmingly people-powered. While competitive, they were not particularly about winning and losing: they brought family and friends together for the uncomplicated purpose of enjoying one another's company while having fun for fun's sake. It was a great time to be a games lover.

> *A manual of Parlour Games has long been a desideratum*
> *among the social and family circles of town and country.*
> — Catharine H. Waterman, *The Book of Parlour Games*, 1853

But along came radio, movies, and then television. People were naturally enthralled by the new technology and the entertainment that these media could deliver — and that was before the marvel of computers. The popularity of the parlour game rapidly waned. Game of Flip the Kipper, anyone? Not while *The Colgate Comedy Hour* is on, and after that there's *I Love Lucy*. Pass me a devilled egg, would you?

Parlour games did, however, live on in popular culture. Some were relegated to children's birthday parties, or to the annual family beach holiday: think Pin the Tail on the Donkey, Blind Man's Buff, Charades. Others appeared in the guise of radio and television game shows, such as *Twenty Questions*, *Celebrity Squares*, and *Wheel of Fortune*. The vast majority of board games on sale at your nearest department store are derived from parlour games: Balderdash, Pictionary, and Battleships, to name but a few. And many computer games have their origins here, too: Nintendo offers a variety of 'parlour games' in its All-Time Classics series.

But, in the beginning, all of these games were played at home — simply, for free, and to the great delight of their participants.

FUN UNPLUGGED

If parlour games died a natural death, why try to revive them? In our parlours, we watch our plasma flat-screen digital TV, and it delivers a perfect picture, crisper than ever before. You can even watch telly on your iPhone, if you are so inclined — perhaps while sitting on the toilet. For something more interactive, there's the Xbox or Wii. As for the World Wide Web, well, you could spend the rest of your life surfing it and never get to the end of the wave.

What is so special, then, about a night of homemade Bingo or a round of Eat Poop You Cat? What kind of loopy Luddites are we?

Here are seven reasons why parlour games are great for modern families:

PARLOUR GAMES ARE FREE

Parlour games are played with equipment that we have to hand. All those games that you thought needed special doodahs, they were having you on. You'll be amazed by how many games you'll recognise in this book in all their naked glory; and you won't have to spend heaps of money on them only to instantaneously lose half the little plastic pieces.

PARLOUR GAMES ARE SUSTAINABLE

We know where the over-consumption of the past century has got us, and we know that we need to find (or rediscover) alternative, 'greener' ways to have fun. Fortunately, we have something to go on: people have been entertaining themselves for thousands of years using very little.

PARLOUR GAMES ENGAGE BODY AND MIND

Much of our modern entertainment is delivered to us in glittering modules that we receive passively, snack and drink to hand. Parlour games require our active participation: we use our minds and bodies to play. Parlour games develop our maths and language skills, deductive thinking, problem solving, strategy, memory, fine and gross motor skills, hand-eye coordination, and general dexterity.

PARLOUR GAMES TEACH LIFE SKILLS

Fundamental life skills are picked up through playing games. You learn in a safe environment about winning and losing, taking turns, and following rules. You become acquainted with the concepts of fairness and justice. You learn resilience and how to manage emotions: elation can turn to despair and back again in five minutes of a good game of Black Lady. You learn about chance and skill, and the way the two interact. You learn how to take on personas and perform in front of others. Playing games is a rehearsal for life.

PARLOUR GAMES NURTURE CREATIVITY

Play is one of the most important wellsprings of creativity, and this is as true of architecture as it is of acting or painting. To make stuff up, we have to play, and games are a lovely and natural way to fuel our imaginations.

PARLOUR GAMES BRING US TOGETHER

According to recent neuroscientific research, too much time spent in front of screens, and too little with other people, alters our brain neurocircuitry so that our ability to read facial expressions and body language is impaired. We're not suggesting that you throw out your TVs (we're not), but there is a need for balance. One of the most powerful and absolutely wonderful things about games is the way that they bring family and friends together.

PARLOUR GAMES ARE FUN

Most important of all, playing parlour games is fun: we do guarantee it. There are games in this book that will make you laugh until you cry. This is really the best, even the only, reason to play. Fun? I hear you echo. That madcap, kind of pointless, brightly coloured stuff? Hell, yes! Just try your hand at Blind Potatoes. But there's also the kicking back, laissez-faire, Gin Rummy kind of fun, a slow smile warming you up from the inside out.

There are endless shades and limitless ways of having fun, but all good fun has the power to bring you into the present moment, to make you feel happy deep inside, and to connect you to yourself and those around you. We realise that playing Farkle won't pay the bills or get the homework done, but it will help you come together in a good way with the people that you love. (See p. 128 on the health benefits of laughter, and p. 91 for an interview with author Bernie DeKoven on the art and science of play.)

If you never did you should. These things are fun and fun is good.
— Dr Seuss

PARLOUR GAMES FOR MODERN FAMILIES

Now you know how we got so caught up in the fun and games and why we think they are important. But what can you expect from this book?

The first thing to say is that, while there are lots of Victorian parlour games in here, and while the playful and resourceful spirit of this period inspired us, we have also included much older and much newer games. People have been playing with marbles for thousands of years, and we couldn't ignore terrific new games like Mafia, invented at a university in Moscow in 1986. Furthermore, not all Victorian parlour games translate to a 21st-century parlour. Proverbs by the Piano? Yeah, right — only if we can Google them first. Or what about a little Snap-Dragon with the kids? Soak raisins in whisky, put them in a dish in the centre of the table, set them alight, then make your fun by snapping out lurid flames between finger and thumb. Can't see the helicopter parents liking that one.

To meet our requirements, the games had to be fun, only use equipment found in a typical home, and be relevant for a modern family. We trawled far and wide to find the games: family, friends, books, the internet, teachers, writers, actors, therapists, and every Tom, Mick, and Carrie we could collar. It could have turned into an encyclopaedia, but we wanted it to be a hand-picked sample, and that it is. In the past year, we have played every single game in this book, so we can personally recommend each one of them. Lots of games didn't make it in, but all those that did get our thumbs up. Obviously, you will find your own favourites.

And there is something in here for everyone. For those who like to play freely with words and ideas, and to demonstrate their powers of deduction, dip into the spoken games. Get wildly creative and cunningly strategic with the fabulous pen and paper games. For those interested in the fascinating interplay of skill and luck, try the dice and card games; or, for those dexterous souls out there with the lightning moves, reach for the knucklebones or marbles. And for the many of us who want to just get out there and play games of pointless grandeur, we are very well catered for here, too.

Please note that the age guide is just that: a guide. There will be four-year-olds ready to play Go Fish, and eight-year-olds who are not. Also, while we have addressed this book to a family audience, the vast majority of these games were designed, in the first instance, to be played by adults, and they are sure to make your next dinner party something really special. This book is for anyone interested in playing, aged three to one hundred and three.

Similarly, the guide to game duration is wildly approximate, and is there just to help with your planning. The length of a game will depend on how many people are playing, how many toilet and snack breaks you take, and how much time is spent pondering, chuckling, and nattering. Apart from the games for two players, or larger groups, estimates are based on four players. For more help with planning, the following chapter, 'Preparing the Parlour', has heaps of practical ideas about how to find the time and space to welcome games into your life — because games should only ever be fun, not a chore you set yourself, or something you do to be a better parent.

Finally, this is not intended as a reference book but rather as a book to *use*. Think of it like a recipe book for delicious, budget family meals. Leave it lying around. Our dream for *Parlour Games for Modern Families* is that, out there, in your parlours, it becomes dog-eared, stained, and scribbled all over. Playing these games has brought us, and our families, enormous pleasure, and we hope it brings you great pleasure, too. Fun for fun's sake: an antidote to modern life.

Give us this day our Daily Game,
and give us our playfulness that we may play together.
— Bernie DeKoven

PREPARING THE PARLOUR

BRINGING GAMES BACK INTO YOUR LIFE

Ah, the luxury of shaking off sleep in the first quiet moments before the rough and tumble of the day starts proper: *Darling, have you seen my mobile? ... Mummy, do you know where my homework book is? ... Can I have chocolate spread in my sandwiches today, pleeeease? ... I don't have any matching socks ... We forgot to do my reader ... Can I watch TV after school?*

And that's just in the first hour. Most of us have some sort of paid or unpaid work to contend with during the day. At the other end of the day, there's usually dinner to be prepared, homework to be completed, a sporting activity or three to be got to and, phew, yes, let's watch some television — I'm pooped.

In the United Kingdom and the United States, each individual watches an average of 28 hours of TV per week. For a person aged 65, this represents approximately 11 years of their life.

There's the frenetic pace with which we live our lives, and then there's the many hours that we spend in front of the television trying to recuperate. In among all the busyness, how do we make time for games?

COME ON IN: WELCOMING GAMES BACK

This is where the kids come in: they can help us to remember what it's like to play, and how to do it at any given opportunity.

According to children's folklorist Dr June Factor, if you are a kid, you will play. Period. Lack of time is no problem. Kids play in the schoolyard, they play while they are waiting for a bus, they play while they are eating their dinner, and they play in their beds when they should be going to sleep. They play clapping games and kissing games, they play ball games and boisterous games, they play chanting games and hiding games. They play all these games naturally and at any given opportunity; they don't have to make the time, they just do it.

Sadly, though, it seems children have less and less chance to just play with each other these days. With electronic entertainment available at every turn; more and more structured activities to run off to; fewer siblings to play with, as the average size of our families declines; and an increase in our anxiety as parents that they shouldn't be bored, not for one second, unstructured and spontaneous play seems to be going out the window. Still, you have to hand it to children: they play, regardless.

Adults, they're a different story. Many of us have forgotten how to play. Being an adult is such a responsible business, what with so many adult-like jobs to do, rent or mortgages to pay, and mouths to feed. But we all played once. Learning how to play again isn't hard. It's like learning how to ride a bike: once you learn, you never forget.

In talking to lots of people about the games they played as children, we found that many had fond memories of their favourites and strong associations with where they played these games: walking up to the 'big house' on the hill to play cards; long, hot afternoons playing Jacks on the floor; or the smell of a dusty blackboard as they played Hangman. Reigniting these memories can help us, as adults, to remember about our own play; and that's as good a place to start as any.

WARMING-UP EXERCISE: THE GAMES I PLAYED

Take time to think back to your own childhood. What games did you play? What are your most fondly remembered ones? Where did you play these games? How did they make you feel? Whom did you play them with?

Once you've shifted the cobwebs to reveal the little gems beneath, talk to your children about your fondest memories of play. Tell them about the countless hours of cards you played with your cousins, or the games of Jacks that you played with your friends, or that night when you played Murder in the Dark.

Invite your children (or nieces or nephews, or grandchildren) to talk about the games they play now. Where do they play them? How are they similar, or different, to the games you played? Can they show you how to play their favourite? Can you show them your all-time favourite?

Taking this a step further, talk to people around you about the games they played. What did 84-year-old Margaret next door play when she was a little girl? What games did your parents play when they were kids? Many, like 91-year-old George on p. 21, may claim not to remember playing much as children; but, once you gently scratch the surface, you will find that everyone played games as a child. Period.

THINGS TO THINK ABOUT WHEN BEGINNING TO PLAY

You can discover more about a person in an hour
of play than in a year of conversation.
— Plato

There's the game, but there are also the players. And they don't always behave the way we would like them to.

The ages, personalities, and inclinations of your fellow players will impact on what sort of games they like and how they play them. John may love active games, but Mary is good at spoken games. Harry likes cards, and Jane, well, she's a good all-rounder. Michelle likes all the rules explained clearly at the start, but Frank likes to learn as he goes. Thankfully, we're all individuals. Some games you can play one-on-one with your children, because you know they love them. Others your children will play with each other, and still others you will play as a family. And then there will be those that you play at the end of the night, when the kids are asleep: playing Nine Men's Morris and Numerology is definitely better for a marriage than surfing the Net.

Often, you will find that younger children quickly get frustrated by rules, either because they don't understand them or they find it too hard to abide by them. Taking turns, playing within a certain time frame, and learning how to lose are difficult concepts to master. They take time. And structured games are great for teaching these skills — just not all at once. So, if a game is getting too hard, or tears seem to break out at every turn, it's time to try something else, or to simply improvise.

Similarly, the needs of older kids should be taken into consideration. If you suggest a game of I Spy, the likely answer will be: 'No thanks ... it doesn't compete with MSN.' Perhaps Celebrity Heads might better fit the bill. We spoke to, and played with, quite a few teenagers in the course of researching this book, and found that they quickly got back into the swing of games. This was both a revelation and a joy. Connecting with young people over a silly game is a wonderful leveller: the vexing issues of staying out late or negotiating the massive mobile phone bill are put to the side. Many teenagers told us that games are still used in some of their classrooms as a teaching tool, and that they made the task of learning more fun. So, don't write teenagers off: invite them into the parlour, and get them interested in some of the games for older kids. They, and you, may be surprised at how interactive these games can be.

CREATING GAMES SPACES

You've had a bit of a think about the games that you played as a child, and you've considered bringing games back into your life. Now, we get down to the practical business of how to create the space and the time in your life for doing just that.

These days, many of our parlours are filled with devices that go beep and bang, bling and boom: the television, the computer, the hand-held electronic game, and the console that's linked to a mind-boggling array of virtual entertainments. Toys are now mass-produced, and are therefore available a lot more cheaply and prolifically than they were in previous generations. It's no wonder, then, that unless we go on holidays where some of these things are absent, family parlour games aren't at the fore of our thinking when it comes to entertainment.

The Victorian parlour — whether it was a dingy, dark room in an inner-working-class suburb, or an airy room with a piano in a leafy middle-class one — had no electronic devices, for a start. And most children did not have a room full of toys. Often, they had to make do with a few, thus the appeal of parlour games.

We are not suggesting for one minute that you ditch the gadgets and revert to a 19th-century lifestyle. This is not only unrealistic but also undesirable: who in their right mind wants to go back to carrying chamber-pots out of the house by hand? What we are doing is inviting you to get into the *spirit* of the

19th-century parlour: switch the electronic devices off every now and then, congregate together, and play. But first, a few words on preparation.

PREPARING THE TOOLS

You can't make a cake without ingredients, and so, too, you can't play some games without the right tools. For most of the games in the book, you will already have the 'tools': most of us have pen and paper lying around. For many of the spoken games, no tools are required at all except your own selves. And for the active games, often, all we need do is get up off our chairs.

Other tools you may need to collect over time (knucklebones from the butcher come to mind), or beg or borrow (marbles, for example). As you collect your tools, it helps to create a space where you can keep them. Perhaps allocate a special box. It might be a wooden one that you find in an op shop, or a shoebox specially decorated by your youngest. Give it a special name — 'Bits when Bored', 'Fits of Family Fun' — as serious or silly as you like.

If a box doesn't work for you, make some space on a shelf, or at the end of the dining-room table, but ensure it is somewhere accessible and within view. In this space, you may have a heap of recycled paper, a jar of pens, a deck of cards, some dice and, of course, this book.

Once you start regularly playing some of the games herein, you may find that your children start dipping into the special games box or fossicking through the games shelf with very little encouragement from you.

CREATING A PHYSICAL SPACE

While many games will be played informally all over the house, it can help to create a designated 'games space'. For card games, it could be the dining-room table; for spoken games, it could be a favourite arm chair. Over time, this inviting space will come to mean family time, a lot of laughter, and even the occasional argument. If it's the dining-room table, make a show of clearing it of detritus and laying it with a hardy tablecloth on which it's okay to spill drinks and scatter peanut shells. If it's the comfy chair in the living room, turn the TV off, switch on the lamps, bring on the hot chocolate, and go for it.

CREATING OPPORTUNITIES FOR GAMES

There is no doubt that, if we could buy time, most of us would be queuing up for it. Unfortunately, we have to work with what we've got. Which is not much.

Fear not: most of the games in this book don't take up a lot of time. The shortest is three minutes long; the longest might span into the wee hours of the night, if the company is right. It is encouraging to know that a fair few of the games in this book, particularly the spoken ones, were played by us in the stolen moments before bed, or while cooking dinner, or during a few quiet minutes when boredom loomed.

Here are our choice ideas for creating opportunities for games in your life, from playing a few quickies to hosting your very own games-night extraordinaire.

TWENTY TIPS FOR CREATING GAMES OPPORTUNITIES BIG AND SMALL

1. Keep *Parlour Games for Modern Families* handy on the coffee or dining-room table, so that you or your children can dip into it for inspiration.
2. Play a spoken-word game when giving the kids a bath, just before the goodnight kiss, or while cooking dinner.
3. Suggest a game of cards or marbles after a weeknight dinner. Grab the required accoutrements, and you are in business.
4. In the sleepy lull after a big lunch with the extended family, play a good group game like Celebrity Heads, or put on a Talent Quest.

5. Put up a little blackboard or piece of paper in the kitchen. Each day, before the kids come home from school, write up a family game that you will try that night. Do this for two weeks. We guarantee that after-school television will soon be relegated to the back burner.

6. Once a week, on the same night each time, have a games hour. Try one old favourite and one new game. Get your kids to draw up a roster and take it in turns to choose their favourite game.

7. Kids restless in the car? Starting to bicker while waiting for a meal in a restaurant? Have a bevy of short games that you can suggest they play anytime, anywhere. Have ready in your bag: paper, a pencil, and some dice.

8. When camping, a deck of cards is *de rigueur*. Don't forget to chuck this book in your rucksack as well. Who knows when the family will feel like a game of Pig?

9. Set yourself and your family a novel task: to play a game from each section of this book within the next month, to play your way through 20 games this summer, or to play one Game of Motion (see p. 77 for these) each week for eight weeks. Beats going on a diet.

10. Make your own knucklebones (recipe on p. 215), and teach your child how to play.

11. Ask an older person to teach your children how to play a particularly complex game of cards, or put aside some time to teach your children some games that you played as a child.

12. Get the kids to make some homemade invitations, and organise a group of friends to come over for a games afternoon or night. Choose between two and six games that are appropriate for the ages of your guests. Bake a jam tart (p. 170), put on a pot of tea (p. 220), and let the fun unfurl.

13. Host a card-games night. Have instructions for simple card games for the kids, while the adults can try more sophisticated card games at another table. Why not get everyone to dress in 1920s' gear? For a subversive, speakeasy feel, whip up some Campari cocktails for the adults and mocktails for the kids, and you're up for a roaring night.

14. If you'd like to wow your guests with your knowledge of movie, book, play, and song titles, hold a Carnelli night. See p. 249 for the game.

15. What about a night of forfeits? Turn to p. 105 and laugh yourself silly at some of the things you can get your guests (and of course, yourself) to do.

I bet you've never seen Peter Smith, little Johnnie's dad from the school, compose and sing a song about pickled eggs.

16. Host a Bingo night, complete with blue-rinse wigs, pots of shandy for the adults, and a bit of raucous 'sixty-six, clickety click' (see p. 70).

17. Does murder appeal? Why not host a dangerous evening of Wink Murder (p. 111), Mafia (p. 118), and Murder in the Dark (p. 117)? Ask your guests to dress as mobsters, and intersperse games with dinner, cocktails, and dancing to add to the intrigue and fun.

18. A formal event, such as a wedding, christening, or 80th birthday, is a great time to play games. Prepare a different game for each table, printed on beautiful, textured paper and sealed in an envelope. Games will set the scene for a fun, relaxing afternoon or evening.

19. Plan a fundraiser at the local pub or scout hall, complete with musty smells and ropes hanging off the rafters. If you like, ask everyone to come in old-fashioned dress (as parlour maids, or a character from a Dickens novel, perhaps). You or your guests will need to bring card tables, cards, dice, pen, paper, and snacks. Have age-appropriate games on the tables for each group. Charge a sensible entrance fee, and donate it to a worthy cause.

20. And, finally, if you're game, why not go into a public place, such as your city square, and play Blind Man's Buff? Watch people's reactions, and then ask them if they'd like to join in. What the heck, just do it for fun.

Whether you use this book to play the odd game here or there on a dull afternoon, or on holidays, when the computerised gadgets don't beckon, or you choose to go for the long, slow burn of games-for-life, as advocated by our fun-loving friend Bernie DeKoven, we implore you: never give up on playing. No matter how old you are.

We leave you with the words of playwright George Bernard Shaw: 'We don't stop playing because we grow old; we grow old because we stop playing.'

PAPER AND PEN? JUST TELL ME WHEN!

GAMES OF WRITING AND DRAWING

The word 'paper' comes from the Greek term for the ancient Egyptian writing material papyrus, which was formed from beaten strips of papyrus plants that were once abundant in the Nile Delta of Egypt. The Egyptians used thin reed brushes or pens made from the sea rush to write on it.

Through the ages, paper has been made from materials including textile waste, bamboo, and even straw. These days, it is made mainly from trees. In the mid-19th century, the process of production was industrialised, and so paper became more readily available. If anything, it is in such abundant supply now that we tend to use it with very little consideration for the environmental consequences. So as to minimise wastage, it doesn't hurt to have a box of recycled paper handy — from computer printouts, or scraps from work — for the games in this section.

The first 'written' games were invented well before paper was commercially available: Nine Men's Morris, for example, has been around since ancient Egyptian times, with boards found etched on clay tiles that date back to that period. Others, such as Consequences, made their appearance in the 16th century; and still others, like Hangman and Doublets, were popular in the 19th century. These games continue to resonate today.

Many of the games that follow can be played with quite young kids, especially those that focus on drawing, like the Mirror Game or Picture Consequences, and those that require simple strategy skills, such as Noughts and Crosses. Others take a bit of clever wordsmithing, like Alphabet Race; more sophisticated strategic moves, such as Nine Men's Morris; or even a bit of numerical acrobatics, like Numerology. Many of the games for younger children build on skills, such as making defensive as well as proactive moves, that will put them in good stead for more sophisticated strategic games later on. And we have even had a bash at making a board game or two: why buy a commercially made game when you can have more fun drawing it up at home?

A lot of the games in this section can be played by two players, so they don't require big groups. In this way, siblings can happily while away an hour on a Sunday afternoon playing, or adults can clear the table and play a soothing game or two after the kids have gone off to bed.

As for the writing implements, we have stated that most games simply require a pen. If your household is anything like ours, where pens (along with socks) have a marvellous way of disappearing, then just make do with whatever else happens to be lying around, such as a crayon, a pencil, or even chalk.

BUT FIRST, A YARN WITH GEORGE ...

Ninety-one-year-old George Perry grew up in the Depression years. One of his first memories is of his dad going off on a horse and cart to catch rabbits in rural Victoria (Australia). The family ate the rabbit meat and dried the skins for the local hat works in town. His mother died when he was aged ten, and he was obliged to leave school and start work at age thirteen. George describes his childhood as 'bloody tough'. He told us about the games he played when was growing up:

> As kids, we played games that didn't cost us anything. We didn't have much money for entertainment. We used to go to the homes of our aunties and uncles, where a pack of cards was the prime item. Ten people could play with a pack of cards, and it would cost you nothing.
>
> We would stand around watching our parents playing, which gave us a bit of insight into the games. The main ones in those days were Euka and 500. Us kids would also play Strip Jack Naked, and Snap, although we didn't often get the deck to ourselves, unless it was pretty knackered.
>
> Later on, in the army, we played Two-Up and Heads and Tails. We would play in the toilets of a night time, because it was the only place with electric lights. I have a good card sense because I'm an observer, and I'm pretty objective. If you can play cards, you can dance, and you can swim, you've got the game by the throat.
>
> At school, my favourite game was Cherry Bobs: you would get the pips of cherries and dry them. We'd take them to school in a cloth bag, and dig a hole against the fence. Then, we would throw them, and whoever got closest to the hole took the pool.
>
> We used to play marbles, too; but marbles you had to buy, and not all of us could afford them. You owned them and you lost them — we used to play for keeps.
>
> The girls used to get the knucklebones from a leg of lamb so they could play Jacks. For those families that could afford it,

they would prefer to buy a leg of lamb over chops, because it went a bit further.

When I was about nine, I won a football. A football was a highly sought-after object, because everyone used to play football with a bit of rolled-up newspaper, tied up with some string. Not many people could afford a real football in those days. As we were going home, everyone was shouting out, 'Georgie, Georgie, give us a kick, give us a kick.'

I really reckon the kids of today have fantastic opportunities. To my mind, every generation of parents tries to make it easier for their kids, but we've got to be careful not to make it too easy. When television came in, I think it gave people false aspirations; it made them envious, always wanting more. So many people are influenced by television and advertising; it's robbed people of the necessity to think. It's a good idea to turn the bloody thing off.

I think the key to life is knowing when to say no to yourself, and kids have got to learn that at some stage. Adversity is not always a bad thing: my childhood was hard, but I don't regret any of it.

GAMES WITH PICTURES

'What is the use of a book', thought Alice, 'without pictures or conversations?'
— from *Alice's Adventures in Wonderland*, Lewis Carroll

The first way in which very young children express themselves on paper is through pictures: they go from indecipherable scribbles to clumsily drawn stick figures, to more or less recognisable scenes that describe the world around them. But, as we get older, for most people, our tendency to draw is usurped by our inclination to write: pictures are relegated to the treasure chest of childish things.

In these games, we encourage you to re-discover the artist within. You might find that children have a thing or two to teach you here. These drawing games help us to convey meanings (Pictures), remind us to use our imagination (Squiggle), and make us laugh (Eat Poop You Cat). Now, that's got to be good for you.

THE MIRROR GAME

This delightful mirror drawing game is simply good fun. What more could you want?

NUMBER OF PLAYERS	2 or more
AGE	5 and up
YOU WILL NEED	A decent-sized mirror, a pen, and paper
PLAYING TIME	5 minutes per drawing

OBJECT OF THE GAME
To draw a picture by looking through a mirror.

HOW TO PLAY
Each player takes it in turn to draw an object on a piece of paper — say, a house, a cat, or a car — but only by looking at its reflection in a mirror. If they are standing, they can lean the paper up against their chest, holding it up with one hand and drawing with the other as they face the mirror. If available, a small mirror can be put up on a table, leaning against a wall; and children can sit down to draw their pictures. Looking at the page is expressly forbidden; players who are waiting their turn need to keep an eagle eye out for such behaviour. The exercise sounds easy, but you will soon discover that it's not.

Once players have mastered a simple animal, they may like to move on to more difficult objects, such as a watch with its hand pointing to a definite time. Children are sometimes frustrated at how hard this is to do, but there is usually a fair bit of laughter when they see the result.

An hourglass can be used to time players, thus producing even more outrageous results.

If children are playing, once they have done a few drawings, a parent or older sibling might judge which is The Best Drawing, The Most Wobbly Drawing, or The Drawing That Was the Closest to Telling the Correct Time! It may be that the prize is to play another fun game (Squiggle, below, is one of our favourites).

SQUIGGLE

This game delighted millions of Australian children who watched the television show *Mr Squiggle* through the years (more on the show below). Mr Squiggle's ability to magically turn a squiggle into a very lovely picture never ceased to amaze viewers.

The origins of this game are grounded in the parlour, well before the advent of television. We believe this simple game will continue to delight little (and re-ignite bigger) imaginations for a very long time to come.

NUMBER OF PLAYERS	2 or more
AGE	4 and up
YOU WILL NEED	Pen and paper
PLAYING TIME	5 minutes per drawing

OBJECT OF THE GAME

To make the most creative drawing you can out of a squiggle.

HOW TO PLAY

If there are two players, each player draws a squiggle on a piece of paper and then swaps these around. The goal is to then make as creative a drawing as possible from the squiggle. In a larger group, an adult can draw the squiggles and distribute these, or children can draw squiggles and swap.

It's amazing what children can see in a line, a circle, or a squiggly shape. Often, they come up with delightfully unexpected drawings.

Once a number of pictures have been drawn, everyone holds up their pictures for all to admire. Small prizes might be awarded for The Most Creative Drawing, or a picture from each player can be stuck up on the fridge for all to view.

This is a great game to set for young children who could do with some 'settling down' time: make a quick squiggle and send a raucous child off to do the most creative, special, and colourful drawing that they can. That should give parents a good ten-minute reprieve to get dinner on.

VARIATIONS

Each player places six random dots on a piece of paper and passes this to the player on their left, whose job it is to make a picture of an animal or a person.

Yet another variation is to start a shape (circle, triangle, or a square, for example) and try to make it into an object. Each player starts with a sheet of drawing paper. One player names a shape. Everyone then has to sketch as many objects as they can think of, using that shape. At the end of five minutes, the person with the most ideas is deemed to be the winner.

DID YOU KNOW?

The ABC's *Mr Squiggle* was one of Australia's longest-running children's series (1959–1999). Mr Squiggle was a marionette puppet who lived on the Moon (93 Crater Crescent). He loved to visit his friends, Rebecca, Bill Steamshovel, and Gus the Snail. Mr Squiggle had a pencil for a nose, and turned viewers' squiggles into recognisable drawings. He did sometimes get very distracted and go for 'space walks', during which he had to be led back to the important task at hand. And, oh, let's not forget grumpy Blackboard, whom Mr Squiggle rested his pictures on; he often called out, 'Oh, hu-rry u-p, hu-rry u-p!'

PICTURE CONSEQUENCES

There are many variations of this game using words (see p. 38), but younger children will enjoy this one because it uses pictures; it's easy, and the results are often very amusing. The element of surprise (to which they have each contributed) gets kids going every time.

NUMBER OF PLAYERS	2 or more
AGE	4 and up
YOU WILL NEED	Pen and paper
PLAYING TIME	5 minutes per round

OBJECT OF THE GAME
To draw the funniest made-up character that you can.

HOW TO PLAY
Each player takes a sheet of paper on which they draw the head of a person or beast — the more creative and ridiculous the drawing, the better. They fold the paper down, leaving only a small part of the neck showing. They pass this down the line, and the next player attaches a body to the neck. That player then folds the paper down again, with only a tiny part of the torso showing, and passes it along for the next player to draw the legs. Finally, the last player draws the feet. When everyone has finished drawing, each piece of paper is unfolded, in turn, and the results are shared around the table, usually to great amusement.

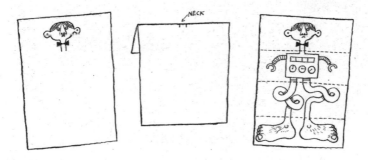

PICTURES

Also known as Quick on the Draw, and the trademarked version, Pictionary, this game relies on trying to communicate your message as quickly as possible through pictures alone. We challenge you to maintain your dignity as urgent hilarity and desperate gesticulation break out.

NUMBER OF PLAYERS	4 or more
AGE	6 and up
YOU WILL NEED	Pen and paper, a stopwatch or watch with a second hand
PLAYING TIME	5 minutes per round

OBJECT OF THE GAME
To guess the meaning of a word or phrase as quickly as possible from a diagram alone.

HOW TO PLAY
The group breaks off into a couple of teams of two or more people. One team writes down a word (in the case of younger players), or a phrase. The phrase could be the title of a book, a movie, or a quote, for example.

The phrase is given to one member of the opposing team, making sure all the while that others in their team don't see what it is. That player then has to convey that meaning to the rest of the team members, using pictures only, and within one minute. As in Charades, certain symbols are used to represent categories. For example:

PLAY

FILM

SONG

QUOTE

BOOK

The number of words in a phrase is indicated with a series of long dashes. No words can be spoken, nor can gestures or audible noises be made. The pictures drawn cannot have any numbers or letters. If a team commits any of these misdemeanours, play reverts to the other group, and no points are granted.

If a correct guess is made within one minute, that team scores one point, and play moves to the opposing team. The team with the most points at the end wins.

The more players you have, the louder this game becomes, as team members feverishly call out their guesses to the person illustrating the word or phrase. And then there's the voyeuristic element: the opposing team gets to have a good laugh at both the drawings and the guesses. A great after-dinner game.

REDONDO

In most of the drawing games so far, you goal is to draw something recognisable. Well, throw that notion out the window. In this game, the goal is to draw something that can't really be deciphered: a nonsense, inexplicable picture whose design it is to confuse. We like it already.

NUMBER OF PLAYERS	3 or more
AGE	6 and up
YOU WILL NEED	Pen and paper
PLAYING TIME	10 to 15 minutes per round

OBJECT OF THE GAME
To be as imaginative as possible in your drawing and captions.

HOW TO PLAY
Put a stack of paper in the middle of the table, where everyone can access it. Each player will also require something to draw with: a pen, pencil, or crayon — whatever is at hand.

Players take a piece of paper and draw a doodle; the doodle can be as wild and doodly as they like. It need not make any sense; in fact, the less sense it makes, the more fun this game is. For example, it can be a geometric shape, something that looks like a puff of air, or a mysterious box — something pretty quick, as you don't have much time for elaborate works of art. As soon as one of the players is done, they place the paper face down in the middle of the table and call out, 'Redondo.' Players then have to stop drawing and also put their doodle face down in the middle of the table. Each of the players then grab any doodle from this pile, making sure that they don't grab their own. They may take some time to look at the drawing and allow its inner meaning to bubble to the surface. Once it has, they need to caption the drawing. The more absurd the caption, the better.

The captioned doodles are now placed in a separate pile, and when everyone has finished the drawing may begin again. The game continues in this way until the company tires of doodling and captioning.

Players then take turns picking from the pile of the titled 'Redondos'. They hold up the work, read the captions, and elaborate on the merits of the work for all to behold, with all the seriousness of an art critic.

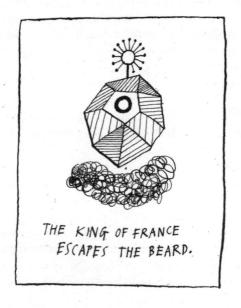

THE KING OF FRANCE
ESCAPES THE BEARD.

EAT POOP YOU CAT

While this game is also known as The Sentence Game, The Paper Game, and Telephone Pictionary, we couldn't go past this great name. It is a cross between Chinese Whispers (p. 262) and Pictures (p. 28), and once you've tried it, we guarantee it will become part of the staple of family favourites.

NUMBER OF PLAYERS	3 or more
AGE	6 and up
YOU WILL NEED	Pen and paper
PLAYING TIME	10 to 15 minutes per round

OBJECT OF THE GAME

To be as imaginative as possible in your drawing and captions.

HOW TO PLAY

Each player has a piece of paper on which they write a phrase at the top, for example, 'Toilet paper was running low on the planet of Uranus.' The more interesting, funny, or unusual the phrase, the more amusing the results of this game will be. Each player draws a small illustration below their caption to convey its meaning. Once all the players have written their caption and illustrated it, they fold the top part of the paper over to cover the caption, but not the illustration.

Each paper is passed to the left, and it is the job of the next player to write a phrase that they think best describes the illustration in front of them. Once again, amusement rather than accuracy is the main premise here — use your imagination. Players then fold the paper over the illustration of the previous player (leaving the phrase showing), and play moves around the group, where another illustration is drawn to describe the phrase.

In this way, the sequence is: phrase, illustration, phrase, illustration, etc. The instructions to this game take a bit of explaining, in our experience. Younger players should be assured that they need not worry about correct spelling and literal descriptions: the aim is to be as silly as you can.

Play can stop when everyone has had a turn, or when you have reached the end of the paper (you may need two pieces of paper stuck together, if you have a bigger group). Children who are not yet literate can be paired up with an older child or adult; a lot of very fervent whispering ensues, as the idea is that no one else knows what you are illustrating or writing.

At the end, each of the players opens up their papers and talks through what they have written and illustrated.

This game is a classic. The first time we played it, one of our children nearly hyperventilated with laughter, and another was scrabbling across the table to see what had been written.

TOILET PAPER WAS RUNNING LOW ON THE PLANET OF URANUS

SPACE TOILET MEETS A STRANGE FLOWER

'THAT'S THE WORST PLANE EVER' SAID DAISY

COW DIDN'T NOTICE THE FLYING SAUSAGES

GAMES WITH WORDS

We love playing with words in the parlour, and there are lots to be had in this section.

Lewis Carroll loved playing with words, too, which is abundantly clear to anyone who has read *Alice's Adventures in Wonderland*. In this section, we tell you a bit more about Carroll (a.k.a. Charles Lutwidge Dodgson) and the games that he invented. We take you through a potted history of telegrams, and show you how to devise some funny ones of your own. And, in the true spirit of the parlour, we tell you about games that are old favourites, such as Consequences, and introduce you to some novel ones, like Legs.

As many of the games in this section rely on a certain level of literacy, they are for slightly older children (starting age five and up), but there's no reason why smaller children can't team up with adults to play.

We leave you with the Irish blessing: 'May you have warm words on a cold evening, a full moon on a dark night, and a smooth road all the way to your door.'

HANGMAN

Also known as Gallows, The Game of Hangin, or Hanger, this game has been played since Victorian times, though some modern readers may find its objective repellent: metaphorically speaking, if you do not guess a word, your man will be hanged. If you find this questionable, then you might prefer the variation.

NUMBER OF PLAYER	2 or more
AGE	5 and up
YOU WILL NEED	Pen and paper (or a blackboard); players require the ability to spell at least simple words
PLAYING TIME	5 minutes per round

OBJECT OF THE GAME

To guess a word so that your man is granted reprieve from being hanged.

HOW TO PLAY

One player, the Hangman, thinks of a word, which he does not share with the other players. He places a series of dashes on the paper or blackboard corresponding with the number of letters in that word. For example, if the word is 'wonderful', nine dashes will be marked.

The other players now call out letters, one by one. If their letter is correct, the Hangman places this on the corresponding dash. If one of the letters is incorrect, the Hangman starts to draw a part of the gallows (one stroke for each wrong letter), starting from the frame and continuing with the person. They also record the letter underneath the gallows, so that players remember not to mention that letter again. In this way, the guessers have 11 'reprieves' before their man is hanged.

Players can call out at any time if they think they know the word. Any player who calls out a correct guess gets to choose the next word.

To make it simple for very young players, choose shorter words that they are very familiar with, such as 'cat' or 'dog'. This is a great exercise for practising words that beginning readers are learning at school, and is a good boost for their confidence in spelling.

For older or more experienced players, longer words or phrases can be chosen, or words with obscure letters, such as x and z. Especially clever players will know that some letters are more common in daily usage than others (we could tell you which, but that would be giving it away now, wouldn't it?). Alternatively, the gallows can be drawn before the game properly begins, giving players fewer guesses.

VARIATION

Instead of a gallows, an apple tree with ten apples can be drawn at the outset. Each of the apples is crossed out as the guesses are used up.

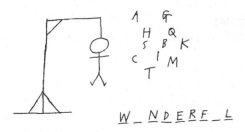

HANGMAN AT BALOOK

The Balook township, population 13, is nestled in the Strzlecki Ranges, in the Australian state of Victoria's South Gippsland. One of our regular family holidays is at the old Balook school house (circa 1915). A game of Hangman often arises spontaneously among the cousins and friends, who mill about by the blackboard, which is conveniently close to the open fireplace and to quite a few packets of marshmallows. As the noise level and dust from the chalk rises so, too, does the apprehension that our man will be hanged. We often wonder: how many children before ours have stood in this very spot, and played the same game, throughout the school's history?

CHATTERBOXES

When our children first bought home a Chatterbox from school, we were each instantly transported back to our own primary school days of making these paper devices, full of fortunes and wishes. If your children haven't learnt how to make Chatterboxes at school by the very organic process of osmosis, here is the formula:

NUMBER OF PLAYERS	2
AGE	6 and up
YOU WILL NEED	Pen and paper (hardy paper usually works best, if you have it), scissors
PLAYING TIME	10 minutes to make Chatterbox, 2 to 3 minutes to play

OBJECT OF THE GAME

To make and play Chatterboxes.

HOW TO MAKE A CHATTERBOX

1. Cut a piece of paper into a square. We find that 20cm x 20cm works best.
2. Fold this in half, and then unfold it again, so that you have a crease down the length of your square.
3. Fold this again in the opposite direction, and open it up again. You will now have two creases that form a cross. For the most precise results, place a dot in the very middle of the cross, where your two creases meet.
4. Fold all four corners of the square into the middle, so that they all meet at your dot. Crease well.
5. Turn your square over.
6. Fold all four corners of this smaller square, so that they meet in the middle, as before. Crease well.
7. Turn your square over, and make the final creases by folding your square in half. Unfold, and then fold in the opposite direction.
8. Open the Chatterbox back, and slip thumbs and fingers into the outside sleeves, so as to move it back and forth.

HOW TO PLAY

This is the bit where you can let your imagination run riot. You will need to write certain things on the outside and inside of your Chatterbox. Here is the traditional method:

Player 1 writes any four numbers (up to 20) on the outside sleeves of the Chatterbox. The number chosen by Player 2 is the number of times the Chatterbox is moved back and forth. On the inside of the Chatterbox are written the names of colours. Player 2 chooses a colour, and the Chatterbox is moved back and forth according to the number of letters in that colour: for example, if the colour is pink, Player 1 moves the Chatterbox back and forth four times, calling out each letter, P-I-N-K, as he goes. Player 2 then chooses a colour again, and the corresponding flap is opened to reveal what is written inside. Traditionally, a fortune is told: 'You will have good luck for the rest of the day', for example.

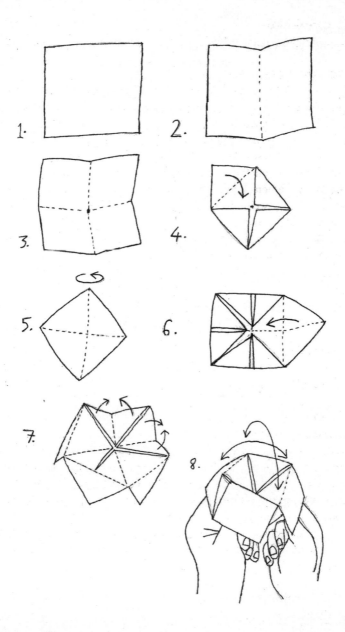

VARIATION

You can use your Chatterbox in all sorts of ways. You may like to use it to reward a winner of a game that you have just played — perhaps by filling it with promises of small gifts (giving out chocolate prizes is always gratifying). Alternatively, issue embarrassing forfeits, such a request to impersonate a lizard (see p. 105 for more on ideas on forfeits). Finally, players can populate it with characters from their favourite book or movie, and ask the other player to tell an amusing story, based on the character that they land on.

CONSEQUENCES

Consequences is a very old game, already well established in the 16th century. It continues to be handed down, generation after generation. Some things just never change: when boy meets girl, the world is bound to talk. A good one for teenagers, in our opinion.

NUMBER OF PLAYERS	2 or more
AGE	6 and up
YOU WILL NEED	Pen and paper
PLAYING TIME	10 minutes per round

OBJECT OF THE GAME

To make up a communal, nonsensical, and amusing boy-meets-girl story.

HOW TO PLAY

Each player starts by writing an adjective at the top of their piece of paper (for example, 'stern', 'lovable', 'cute'). Then, they fold the paper down over itself, and pass it to the player on their left. A man's name is added (say, 'Mr Biggles', 'Mr Groovy', 'Sir Table'), and then the paper is folded over and passed on again.

In this way, each player adds a piece of information, which is duly covered and passed on. While it can vary, the following information is usually included:

1. Adjective
2. Man's name
3. An adjective describing the woman he met
4. Woman's name
5. Where they met
6. What he gave her
7. What he said to her
8. What she said to him in reply
9. What the consequence was
10. And what the world said (the outcome)

At the end of the round, all the pieces of paper are opened up and read out.

For example, the story might read as follows: 'Stern Sir Table met vivacious Suzy at the park. He gave her a box, and said to her, "I love you." She said, "You are a nerd." The consequence was that he kissed her, and the world said, "Oh dear."'

To make the story even more silly and convoluted, you can add information after you state their name, like what each was wearing and doing, and what each was thinking just before they spoke. Play a few times and really get into the swing of things; the possibilities are endless.

VARIATIONS
Consequences using poetry
The same concept applies here but, instead of a story, poetry is used. This makes it considerably harder, though the rewards are worth it:

Everyone has a pen and a sheet of paper on which they write the name of a potential poem. Players pass their sheet of paper to the player on their left, who proceeds to write the first line of the poem. They then fold over the sheet so that the title is covered but the first line is still visible. These are passed on to the left again, and play continues until all players have written a line of poetry inspired by the last line visible on the paper.

These are unfolded at the end of play (it is best to decide at the outset how many lines will be written) and read out, usually to great amusement. If you get really good at this, you can try limericks or rhyming formats.

Book Reviews
Yet another variation of this game, for those with literary leanings, involves players writing a book review. Players state the made-up name of a book (the more ridiculous, the better), the author's name, their opinion on the merits of the book, and (usually in complete contrast) their critique of the book. For example:

Murder in Maroochydore
by Shyster Sly
is an epic drama of mind-boggling proportions.
Both finely executed and ridiculously stupid,
this is the first time we have seen such extraordinary drivel.

NEWSPAPERS

Fish and chips on the foreshore, going to the drive-in, walks in the bush: can the editor-in-chief get all these stories down in time for their family's newspaper deadline? Can she come up with engaging headlines? And how will she encourage contributions?

Best played over a longish family holiday away, this lovely old game is also a good exercise on school holidays where boredom threatens to wreak havoc. It's a great way for budding young editors to strut their stuff, and the bonus is that the family newspaper can be kept as a memento.

NUMBER OF PLAYERS	2 or more
AGE	6 and up
YOU WILL NEED	A box (a shoebox or any other small box); markers; clean A4-sized paper; paste or sticky tape
PLAYING TIME	Preparation, 1 hour; game played over one week

OBJECT OF THE GAME

To make a family newspaper over a period of a week.

HOW TO PLAY

One player volunteers to be editor-in-chief. Their key role is to ensure that the family newspaper comes out in time. They have precisely one week (or any other reasonable amount of time). They need to inspire family members to contribute stories, pictures, and other paraphernalia to go into the newspaper. When will the deadline be? How much time will they need to bring the stories together? What will the newspaper be called? These are all questions that can be discussed between newspaper 'staff' at the outset.

If there are other budding staff who want to join the newsroom, more roles can be assigned: assistant editor, journalist, or girl Friday. If there is much interest in the editor-in-chief role, players can take turns at it. All the roles will need to be clearly defined from the start: adults can explain the differences between them, and kids might like to talk about what each of them will be in charge of (great practice for later life in the workforce).

The first job is to make a communal box in which the 'copy' for the newspaper will go. This can be an old shoebox or a cardboard box that is lying around the house. Cut a slot into the top of the box for your materials to go in. If you like, decorate the box with pictures, stickers, or whatever takes your fancy. Clearly label the box 'family newspaper' (or, better still, the name of your family newspaper) and place it in a central spot, so that no one forgets that it's there.

Next, it is the job of each family member to put things in the box that will form the content of the newspaper: a story about a day on the beach, a ticket stub from the movie that you went to, or a brochure from the special attraction that you visited. Any two-dimensional snippet can be put in the box (three-dimensional seashells might be a bit hard to integrate into newspaper copy: a drawing will have to suffice). When sitting around making the box, it helps to talk about the sort of things that can go into it. The editor-in-chief will then need to ensure that people are regularly contributing.

At the end of the week, the editor-in-chief and helpers have a project: to make a family newspaper using all the things in the box. They will need to think about headlines, what the feature story will be, how to lay out each page, and what illustrations will accompany each story. They may choose to include jokes and puzzles. If there are not enough things in the box, the editor-in-chief may have to growl at the contributors for some last-minute contributions. A bit of newspaper-office-like chaos should prevail as the newsroom staff rush to meet their deadline.

Now for the unveiling: make yourselves a cuppa, sit down, and go through the family newspaper, reflecting on the week that has been.

DID YOU KNOW?

A 'girl Friday' is an office assistant who has to carry out a wide variety of (usually mundane) tasks. While the term has a somewhat derogatory meaning in modern-day circles, the role was brought to its most amusing and glamorous heights in the 1940s' movie *His Girl Friday*, with Cary Grant (playing hard-boiled editor for *The Morning Post*) and Rosaline Russell. It is an hilarious and fast-paced account of life in newspapers: a good one to seek out and watch for inspiration before embarking on a game of Newspapers.

CATEGORIES

Some may remember this as the 'Boy Girl' game, others will know it as the trademarked Scattergories. The aim is to use the letters of the alphabet to think of words in a particular category, and it can be adapted to suit those of all ages and interests.

NUMBER OF PLAYERS	2 or more
AGE	7 and up
YOU WILL NEED	Pen and paper, stopwatch or watch with a second hand
PLAYING TIME	5 to 10 minutes per round

OBJECT OF THE GAME
To think of words starting with a designated letter in a particular category.

HOW TO PLAY
Along the side of each player's page, up to eight categories are written down. Any categories can be chosen, and players can take it in turns to choose these.

Examples of the most basic of these, which are more suitable for younger players, are: boy's name, girl's name, animal, country, colour, and television program. For older players and adults, these categories could include books, poets, rivers, bands of the 1980s, parts of the body, or whatever else is of interest.

A letter is then chosen at random by one of the players, usually by landing their finger on a letter on the page of a book or dictionary without looking.

Each of the players then has to write down words under each of the category headings, starting with that letter. When the first player finishes, the other players have to put down their pens. Alternatively, you can give all players a time limit of three minutes. Each player then reads out their words in turn.

Category	F
Book title	Flaws in the Glass
River	Franklin
Dog breeds	French bulldog
1980s' band	Frankie Goes to Hollywood
Body parts	Fibula

There are various ways in which this can be scored, but the simplest is that players receive two points for any (undisputed) words that no one else has; one point if they have the same word as another player; and no points if they have a blank or a word that is correctly disputed.

VARIATIONS

Write a random five-letter word at the top of the page (say, 'grand'), and think of words for each category that start with the letters in that word. A time limit of five minutes will need to apply to give each player time to think of words. Alternatively, everyone has to stop after the first player finishes all the categories.

Category	G	R	A	N	D
Boy's name	George	Rory	Adrian	Nicholas	Dimitra
Girl's name	Gina	Rebecca	Alice	Nelly	Dolores
Country	Greece	Romania	Australia	Netherlands	Denmark
Colour	Green	Red	Amber	Neutral	Desert sand

Alternatively, you can list a name at the top of a paper (say, Joshua) and, under each letter, list as many names as you can think of that start with that letter (for example, under 'j', you might have Jack, Jill, Jacob, James, etc).

Continue this for each subsequent letter.

Finally, choose a category (say, 'body parts'), and work your way through the alphabet to find things in that category starting with each letter of the alphabet. For example, Adam's apple, brain, capillaries ...

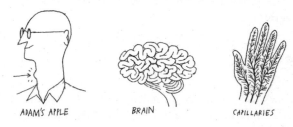

ADAM'S APPLE   BRAIN   CAPILLARIES

ANAGRAMS

An anagram is simply a word that is jumbled up to make another word, or words. A simple example is a word like 'dog', which is an anagram of 'god'. This is a fun and challenging game that can be adapted easily for younger and older players.

NUMBER OF PLAYERS	2 or more
AGE	8 and up
YOU WILL NEED	Pen and paper
PLAYING TIME	5 minutes per round

OBJECT OF THE GAME
To guess the original word.

HOW TO PLAY
Players decide on a category, such as 'animals' or 'countries'.

Each player thinks of something from the chosen category and turns it into an anagram, writing it down on a piece of paper; for example, if the country is 'China', the anagram provided may be 'chain'.

The anagrams are then swapped, if there are two players, or passed to the left, if there are more than two players. The first player to correctly guess the word shouts it out and wins that round, and a new word is jumbled up.

As players get better at this, or for older players, the categories can get more specific, for example, 'James Bond movies' or 'Italian foods'. Think 'Dreamers invade roof', from '*Diamonds Are Forever*', or 'Hospitable gent goes', from 'Spaghetti Bolognese', and you start to get a feel for the possibilities of this game.

ACROSTICS

This game is not what you get when you cross two sticks together. An acrostic is a puzzle in which the first letters of each line spell out a word. For example:

NUMBER OF PLAYERS	2 or more
AGE	8 and up
YOU WILL NEED	Pen and paper
PLAYING TIME	10 minutes per round

GREAT!
AMUSING!
MOREISH!
EXCELLENT!
SO GOOD!

OBJECT OF THE GAME
To guess the acrostic from the clues provided.

HOW TO PLAY
Each player thinks of a word in an agreed category (say, a country). They then write down a clue for each letter of that word. The clues can be simple for younger players, or made more difficult for older players.

For example, if the answer was 'Austria', the clues might be as follows:

A tiny insect that crawls on the ground:	**A**nt
When something is not over, it is:	**U**nder
When someone is a bit weird, they are:	**S**trange
To go from one destination to another:	**T**ravel
The colour of blood is:	**R**ed
People in Greenland once lived in:	**I**gloos
The Italian word for 'love' is:	**A**more

The first player to correctly guess the word wins that round. Play continues with another acrostic, using the same or different category. The player with the most points at the end wins the game.

ALPHABET RACE

This word game will be sure to appeal to lovers of the commercial board game Scrabble. It can be adapted to suit younger wordsmiths, as well as appealing to older children and adults as it stands.

NUMBER OF PLAYERS	2 or more
AGE	8 and up
YOU WILL NEED	Pen and paper
PLAYING TIME	15 to 20 minutes

OBJECT OF THE GAME
To get rid of all the letters of the alphabet as fast as possible.

HOW TO PLAY
Each player writes all the letters of the alphabet on a sheet of paper that they keep in front of them.

Another piece of paper is placed in the middle of the group, and a grid (ten by ten), as per the illustration on the next page, is drawn.

At the toss of a coin, one player goes first, writing a word either vertically or horizontally, using letters from their alphabet. They then cross the corresponding letters off their own sheet. Each player can only use the letters that they choose once, so players cannot make words using double letters, for example, 'kissing'.

The next player places a word on the grid, intersecting with the first player's word. Each player continues to place words down, in turn, with a view to using all their letters as quickly as possible.

C	O	N	S	I	D	E	R	
				I				
				S				
				G				
				R		Z		
			F	A	T	A	L	
				C		N		
				E		Y		

It will soon become apparent to players that, as they use up their vowels, and as there is less space on the paper, it becomes harder to get rid of your letters. Letters x, y, and z are particularly pesky.

Players can pass if they don't have a word, in the hope that, when the next word is placed, there will be a new opening.

Play continues until one player gets rid of all their letters (the adults in our families have never succeeded, but those cleverer than us may well manage it), or when players agree to stop because they cannot use any more letters. In this case, the person with the fewest number of letters wins.

VARIATION

To make this game more accessible for younger players, you may agree at the outset to have two sets of vowels, or even to double the whole alphabet.

LEGS

Have you ever stopped to think how many things have legs? A sofa, a spider, a soldier, and a story are all words starting with 's' that have (or could have) 'legs'. As does a sand chair and a stranger. And what about a string quartet? As you can imagine, this game encourages a fair bit of lateral thinking.

NUMBER OF PLAYERS	3 to 10
AGE	8 and up
YOU WILL NEED	Pen and paper; a watch with a second hand, or an egg timer
PLAYING TIME	5 to 10 minutes per round

OBJECT OF THE GAME
To think of the most things that might, or do, have legs.

HOW TO PLAY
One player chooses a letter at random. Players have three minutes to make as big a list as they can of things starting with that letter that have legs. The idea is to be as creative as possible. Unusual entries will be rewarded. For younger players, five minutes may be required.

One player then reads out their list. The other players (including the one reading out) cross out any words that are on their own list. Each player takes a turn to read out their list, and the same process follows: any words that players have in common are struck out.

All players add up the remaining words on their list, and the person with the most words wins that round. Another round can then be started with another letter.

VARIATION
This game can also be played by listing as many celebrities as players can think of (or any other single category of their choice, for that matter), starting with a designated letter. Scoring follows in the same way as for Legs.

SOLDIER

SOFA

SPIDER

CROSSWORD

NUMBER OF PLAYERS	2 or more
AGE	8 and up
YOU WILL NEED	Pen and paper
PLAYING TIME	15 minutes

OBJECT OF THE GAME

To make the most words that you can, placing letters either vertically or horizontally.

HOW TO PLAY

Each player has a piece of paper on which they draw their own grid. For younger players, a six by six grid will suffice, but for older players a ten by ten grid will make for more interesting play.

A player is selected to go first, and he calls out a letter of the alphabet. Once the letter is called, it is written down in a square of each player's choosing on their respective grids. It is then the next player's turn to call out a letter. The goal is for players to make as many words as they can, either vertically or horizontally, using these letters. If there are two words on a line, they must be separated by a space (which you can shade in), so as to distinguish them from each other. Generally, it is better to make many short words than a few long ones. While you can join two words to make them one longer word, you would only get one point for this. However, three points are awarded for a word that spans the whole length of the grid.

Words should be more than two letters, and should not be abbreviations or proper nouns. Once a letter is in place, it cannot be changed.

The game is over when the grid is full. Scoring then begins, with one point awarded for each word made. Happy crosswording!

DICTIONARY

Also know as Fictionary, Spoof Words, or the trademarked Balderdash, this great game not only helps you learn new words but also tests the ability of players to devise and deliver wacky definitions for obscure words while keeping a straight face.

NUMBER OF PLAYERS	2 to 12
AGES	9 and up
YOU WILL NEED	A dictionary, pen, and identical pieces of paper
PLAYING TIME	10 minutes per word

OBJECT OF THE GAME

To pull one over your opponents with plausible definitions for obscure words.

HOW TO PLAY

One person (the 'reader', if you like) uses the dictionary to look up a word that they believe will be unknown to most people. He states the word to the group, and if anyone knows what the word means, a new word is chosen. He writes down the real definition on a piece of paper. All the other players then set about making up a definition for the word, which they write down on their piece of paper. For example:

Word: *mirza*
Jo: 'A mermaid crossed with a pizza.'
Marian: 'A person who sleepwalks.'
John: 'A person who smells.'
Actual meaning: *A royal prince*

MIRZA

All the definitions are given to the reader and mixed in with the real definition. He then reads all these out to the rest of the players, while trying to keep a straight face. Each player then has to guess which definition they believe is the correct one. The game is scored as follows:

If a player guesses the correct meaning, they get two points.
If a player's definition gets a vote from others, they get one point.
If no one guesses the real definition, the reader gets two points.

Play then rotates around the group, giving everyone a chance to be the reader. The player with the most points at the end wins.

VARIATION

There are a number of ways to play this game, but one simple way is to have a player choose an obscure word from the dictionary and make up three definitions on the spot. Then, they share these with the other players, along with the real definition. The person with the dictionary gets one point for every guess that is incorrect, and the dictionary is passed on to the next player. The person with the most points at the end of the game wins.

TELEGRAMS

> *Wire telegraph is a kind of a very, very long cat. You pull his tail in*
> *New York and his head is meowing in Los Angeles.*
> — Albert Einstein

In this electronic age, where information travels across the world from one computer to another in a matter of seconds, the idea of telegrams is quaint. For those of you who have no idea what we're talking about, read on before you play this one.

DID YOU KNOW?

For more than 150 years, many significant messages of joy, sorrow, and success came in hand-delivered envelopes known as telegrams.

A telegram was usually sent by a telegraph operator (or telegrapher) using Morse code, and was a quick way to convey information over long distances. One of the biggest companies managing these came into being in 1851: The Western Union Telegraph Company.

The first telegram was sent by Samuel Morse, inventor of the Morse code, from Washington to Baltimore on 26 May 1844, to his partner Alfred Vail. It read, 'WHAT HATH GOD WROUGHT?'

Most telegraph companies charged by the word, so customers had good reason to be as brief as possible. This gave telegram prose a snappy, brisk style, and the frequent omission of pronouns and articles often made them poetically ambiguous.

Telegrams reached their peak popularity in the 1920s and 1930s, when it was cheaper to send a telegram than to place a long-distance telephone call. Punctuation was extra, while the four-character word 'stop' was free, so people would save money by using the word 'stop' instead of fullstops.

The Western Union Company delivered its very last telegraph in 2006. The last ten telegrams included birthday wishes, condolences on the death of a loved one, notification of an emergency, and several messages from people just trying to be the last to send a telegram.

But, fear not, the telegram is not yet dead: the innovative mob at telegramstop.com have recently revived it, using the internet as a conduit for sending telegrams on original paper stock. A fine marriage of old and new, we say.

NUMBER OF PLAYERS	2 or more
AGE	9 and up
YOU WILL NEED	Pen and paper, stopwatch or watch with a second hand
PLAYING TIME	5 minutes per round

OBJECT OF THE GAME

To write the funniest message in the snappy style of a telegram, using each letter of a designated word as the starting letter of the words in your telegram (like an acrostic, see p. 46).

HOW TO PLAY

Players choose a long word (for example, 'consequences'), or take it in turns to state up to 12 random letters.

Players must then compose a sensible telegram using those letters in the order that they were selected or appear in the chosen word. If players wish, the first and last letters can be the name of the recipient and the sender respectively. Players may use the word 'stop' to indicate a fullstop, and don't need an 's' in their word to do so.

For example, here is a telegram using the word 'consequences':

'Come Over Next Saturday stop Esther Quit stop Underpants Everywhere stop No Chance Ever Succeeding stop'

Set a time limit of two minutes for each telegram. The writer of the best telegram is deemed the winner. You may need to have an objective bystander to judge. Not only will your skills be honed with each successive round, but the standard (and humour) of your telegrams will also increase. How much delightfully ambiguous news can you deliver in a short amount of time?

VARIATION

Instead of a telegram, can you draft a 26-word sentence using all the consecutive letters of the alphabet at the start of each word? For example:

'A Big Cat Dodged Extremely Fast Goats, Having Interviewed Jackals ...'

The longest sentence to be written down within two minutes wins — unless you want to judge this on the silliest sentence. Ah, what the heck, just do it for a laugh.

DOUBLETS

Not only did Lewis Carroll give us *Alice's Adventures in Wonderland* and other children's stories, but he was also the inventor of the word game Doublets. For more on Carroll and the many things he created, see below. For more on how to bend your brain into a frenzy of wordsmithing, stay here.

NUMBER OF PLAYERS	1 or more
AGE	9 and up
YOU WILL NEED	Pen and paper
PLAYING TIME	5 to 10 minutes per doublet

OBJECT OF THE GAME

To turn one word into another by changing one letter at a time.

HOW TO PLAY

Two related words of the same length are chosen, such as 'head' and 'tail'. The aim of the game is to change only one letter at a time, so as to travel from one word to the next via interposing words.

Using Carroll's own example, the word 'head' may be changed into 'tail' by interposing the words 'heal, teal, tell, tall'. He called the given words 'a doublet', the interposed words 'links', and the entire series 'a chain'. For example:

```
H  E  A  D
h  e  a  l
t  e  a  l
t  e  l  l
t  a  l  l
T  A  I  L
```

The links should be words that can be found in a standard English dictionary, and proper nouns are not allowed.

This game can be played alone or in a group. At any rate, the aim is always to get to the answer in the fewest number of moves. You may choose to have a five-minute time limit. The person to get to the answer in the fewest number of moves within that time limit wins that round. Novice players may find that even being able to solve the puzzle at all (no matter the number of steps) is an achievement in itself.

For younger players, start with three-letter words: say, turning 'cat' into 'dog'. And for those word fanatics, try four- or five-letter words.

LEWIS CARROLL AND DOUBLETS

'Who in the world am I? Ah, that's the great puzzle.'
— from *Alice's Adventures in Wonderland*, Lewis Carroll

Lewis Carroll, the creator of popular children's books *Alice's Adventures in Wonderland* and *Through the Looking Glass, and What Alice Found There*, was a mathematician, logician, theologian, and photographer whose real name was Charles Lutwidge Dodgson (1832–1898). Not only did he write books for children, but his texts on mathematics for adults have also been dusted off and reappraised in recent times. Suffice to say, he was a man of many talents.

According to Morton Cohen, in *Reflections in a Looking Glass*, the man himself was about 'six feet tall, slender, had either gray or blue eyes (observers disagree), wore his hair long, and carried himself upright … almost as if he had swallowed a poker'. He didn't wear spectacles, but was known to use a magnifying glass freely. He wore a tall silk hat and dressed in clerical black, except when he took the 'real' Alice (Alice Liddell, daughter of his friend Henry George Liddell, Dean of Christ Church) and her sisters rowing on the river, in which case he wore white flannel trousers and a white straw hat. The story of *Alice's Adventures in Wonderland* was born on one such journey, and was written down at the urging of Alice herself.

He preferred to give un-birthday presents (because he could give them so many more times in the year), Tuesday was his lucky day, and it is said that he knew instinctively how to evoke peals of laughter from children.

Among his many varied interests, he was, throughout his life, fascinated by puns, acrostics, anagrams, riddles, and all sorts of mathematical games and puzzles. Among the games that he invented were Doublets (initially titled Word-Links), Mischmasch, A Tangled Tale, The Game of Logic, Syzygies, and Lanrick. Many of these were published in books and periodicals at the time, as well as being shared with the many children he knew.

Even in the choosing of his pen name, his love of wordplay

prevailed. Lutwidge chose his pen name by taking his Christian names and translating them into Latin, before reversing the order and turning them back into English. So, 'Charles Lutwidge' became 'Carolus Ludovicus' which, when reversed, became 'Lewis Carroll'.

It is said that he concocted the game of Doublets on Christmas Day in 1877 for 'two little girls who found nothing to do'. It made its first appearance in the pages of the magazine *Vanity Fair* in 1879 and, subsequently, small books of Doublets were printed.

The game is still prevalent today in the back sections of many magazines and newspapers. The goal continues to be to get from one word to the next in the shortest number of 'links'.

So, in the spirit of Lewis Carroll, can you make MORE into LESS, put MILK into PAIL, change MICE into RATS, transform a BEAR into a BULL, go from HATE to LOVE, make LOST into FIND, put INK into PEN, move HAND to FOOT, turn FOUR into FIVE, revive the DEAD into LIVE, shrink a DOOR into a LOCK, turn SLEEP into DREAM, obtain from a BANK a LOAN, make WHEAT into BREAD, or turn TEARS into a SMILE?

GAMES OF STRATEGY

A strategy is a plan of action designed to achieve a particular goal. In games, that goal is usually to win. The word strategy has military connotations, and it derives from the Greek word *stratos*, meaning 'army'.

In contrast to its warlike associations, we have found the process of playing many of these games quite meditative: quietly concentrating on your next move, at the expense of all other thought, focuses your energies, stills your breathing, and brings you into a different space.

NOUGHTS AND CROSSES

Also known as Tic-Tac-Toe or Hugs and Kisses, this deceptively simple game is a bit like a nice wine: left longer, it matures with age. Whether very young kids use it to while away a few minutes, or older kids (or adults) systematically work out a foolproof way to win, it is sure to keep them amused, so long as a scrap of paper and a writing implement are at hand.

NUMBER OF PLAYERS	2
AGE	4 and up
YOU WILL NEED	Pen and paper
PLAYING TIME	2 to 3 minutes per game

OBJECT OF THE GAME
To get three noughts (O) or three crosses (X) in a row, vertically, horizontally, or diagonally.

HOW TO PLAY

Draw a grid using two parallel horizontal lines, and intersect this with two parallel vertical lines. You will now have a grid with nine spaces, which each player takes turns filling in with their assigned symbol, either a nought or a cross.

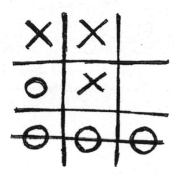

Decide who will be crosses and who will be noughts (in our families, the youngest player usually chooses, or we flip a coin). Also, decide who will go first; again, it might be useful to take it in turns, or suggest that whoever lost the last round gets the first turn in the next round. Being the first to place your mark gives you a slight advantage.

Each player then gets a turn to place their chosen mark in one of the spaces, with a view to getting three noughts or crosses in a row, vertically, horizontally, or diagonally.

This game challenges young players to think defensively, by blocking the other player from getting three in a row, and proactively, so that they get their own three in a row.

Our tactical tip: always place your mark in a corner, and then place your next mark in another corner (irrespective of what the other player does), thus giving yourself two chances to draw a line. There must be a mathematical law for why this is so, but it is beyond us; we just enjoy this game because it is quick and fun. You can't argue with that.

Identical grids to the Noughts and Crosses grid have been found scratched and etched into surfaces all over the ancient Roman Empire, and the game has been played in the United Kingdom for many centuries.

There was a resurgence of interest in the game when British professor of computer science A. S. Douglas developed the first software program to play Noughts and Crosses against the EDSAC machine, a computer that had been built at Cambridge University in 1949.

When winning combinations are considered, there are 255,168 possible games of Noughts and Crosses. Told you it was simple.

SOS

This game is similar to Noughts and Crosses, with an extra layer of complexity.

NUMBER OF PLAYERS	2
AGE	6 and up
YOU WILL NEED	Pen and paper
PLAYING TIME	10 minutes per game

OBJECT OF THE GAME

To spell out 'SOS' (this signal means 'save our souls', and is the conventional Morse code call made by a ship in distress) as many times as you can, vertically, horizontally, or diagonally.

HOW TO PLAY

A grid is drawn: say, eight by eight squares, but it can be more or less, depending on how long you want the game to last. Each player gets a turn at writing either an 'S' or an 'O' in one of the squares on the grid, with a view to getting an 'SOS' sequence. If they do, they can draw a line through it and take another turn. The opponent aims to do the same thing, and it may be that they put a circle around, rather than crossing through, their SOS, so that it can be distinguished from the other player's SOSs. (An alternative is to use different coloured pens.) Once the grid has been filled up, the player with the most SOSs wins. The game ends in a draw if players score equally or not at all.

PADDOCKS

Also known as Dots and Boxes, Squares, or The Dot Game, this is a deceptively simple game. It can be played by younger players without too much deference to strategy, or by older players, who can play it using defensive and proactive moves.

NUMBER OF PLAYERS	2 to 4 players
AGE	6 and up
YOU WILL NEED	Pen and paper
PLAYING TIME	10 minutes per game

OBJECT OF THE GAME
To close off the most squares on a grid.

HOW TO PLAY
Make a grid of dots on a piece of paper — a square of five by five dots is good for beginners. A square of ten by ten dots can be prepared for more expert players, or if you have more than two players.

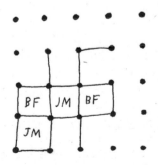

Players take it in turns to draw a vertical or horizontal line from one dot to any of its neighbouring dots. The player who joins up a fourth line, so as to form a box, initials that box. They then get to have another turn, drawing one more line. If, subsequently, they form another box, they get to place another line, and so on. If they can't form any more boxes, play reverts to the other player.

As the game progresses, a series of boxes can be made quite quickly — often referred to as a 'chain'. When chains start to be formed, players need to think not only about the best way to form their own boxes, but also about how to go into damage control, so that the other player doesn't claim a series of boxes in quick succession. At the end of the game, the person with the most boxes (indicated by a tally of their initials) wins the game.

SPROUTS

Sprouts was invented by mathematicians John Horton Conway and Michael S. Paterson at Cambridge University in 1967. No doubt they played this on the back of a napkin, whiling away a few minutes before getting back to their students. At any rate, that's our preferred method of playing.

NUMBER OF PLAYERS	2
AGE	7 and up
YOU WILL NEED	Pen and paper
PLAYING TIME	5 minutes per game

OBJECT OF THE GAME
To be the last to join one dot to another.

HOW TO PLAY
Players place two or more dots randomly on a piece of paper. The more dots that are placed, the longer the game.

Player 1 draws a line between any two of the dots (or from a dot back to itself). It doesn't matter if this line is short or long, straight or winding. Player 1 then places a dot in the middle of the line they have just drawn, in effect, splitting that line into two shorter lines. Player 2 then 'sprouts' a line from any one dot on the page, so as to join with another dot, and places a dot in the middle of their own line. Play continues in this way, with lines sprouting and dots being placed somewhere along these. The lines could keep sprouting forever, and this game would be pointless, but for a couple of rules:

1. A line must not cross over any other line, or over itself.
2. No dot can have more than three lines attached to it. In this way, a new dot placed in the middle of a line has, in effect, two lines attached to it.

Play ends when there are no more possible moves to be made. The winner is the last player to draw their line.

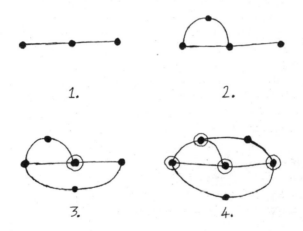

VARIATION

Each player writes down the numbers one to 21, at random, on a piece of paper, so that there are two sets of numbers from one to 21 scattered across the paper, in no particular order. Each player then takes it in turns to join each of the numbers up: the ten with the ten, the 19 with the 19, and so on. Once again, lines are not allowed to cross each other. A player has lost when there is no possible way to join the numbers without crossing over, or colliding with, another line.

BATTLESHIPS

It is said that this game was developed by British prisoners of war during the First World War. This game also has its commercial spin-offs, as with many a game that originated from humble beginnings. It has continued to appeal to the imaginations of generations of children since then.

NUMBER OF PLAYERS	2
AGE	8 and up
YOU WILL NEED	Pen and paper
PLAYING TIME	15 minutes

OBJECT OF THE GAME
To be the first to destroy the 'enemy' fleet.

HOW TO PLAY
Each player draws two ten by ten grids. On the left hand side of the grid, players number the squares from one to ten. Along the top of the grid, they place the letters 'A' to 'J'.

Each player uses one grid for their home fleet, and another for the enemy fleet of their opponent. For the moment, the enemy-fleet grid stays blank.

Each player has a fleet of ships consisting of the following:

One Battleship (equivalent to four squares)
Two Cruisers (each equivalent to three squares)
Three Destroyers (each equivalent to two squares)
Four Submarines (each equivalent to one square)

Each player places their ships on their home grid, by using the letters 'B', 'C', 'D', and 'S' to represent each type of vessel. They must keep their home grid hidden from the other player, perhaps by using a 'screen', such as a book, between them. The letters can be placed vertically or horizontally. Each ship must be made up of consecutive squares. No two ships can touch each other, even by a corner. For example:

HOME FLEET

	A	B	C	D	E	F	G	H	I	J
1										
2		B	B	B	B					
3										
4	S				C					S
5			D		C					
6			D		C		S			
7										
8		D	D							
9							C	C	C	
10	S									

ENEMY FLEET

	A	B	C	D	E	F	G	H	I	J
1										
2										
3										
4										
5										
6										
7										
8										
9										
10			X							

After deciding who will go first (a coin toss should do it), each player takes a turn at guessing where their opponent's enemy fleet might be by calling out a reference (say, 'ten, C'). If no ships are placed there, their opponent calls out 'miss'. A miss is marked as an 'X' on the equivalent square (in this case, 'ten, C') of the enemy-fleet grid (as above). If it is a hit, the letter of the vessel hit is added to the enemy-fleet grid. The other player then has their turn to guess the location of their opponent's enemy fleet. All hits must be declared, as well as the type of vessel hit. In this way, players start to work out where the enemy fleet is placed, and can make a series of directed hits to eliminate them.

The player who hits all the enemy fleets first is the winner.

TAPATAN

This Filipino game is closely related to Noughts and Crosses, and variations of it are played in Ghana, France, and the United States. Tapatan seems a simple game at the outset, but there are some 1680 ways for players to put each of their three pieces on the board. We find this game most meditative.

NUMBER OF PLAYERS	2
AGE	6 and up
YOU WILL NEED	Pen and paper, two sets of three counters (each set of different colours)
PLAYING TIME	5 to 10 minutes per game

OBJECT OF THE GAME
To place all three of your counters in a row.

HOW TO PLAY
Draw up a board on a piece of paper, as per the illustration below.

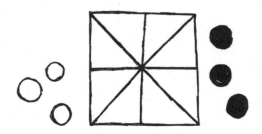

Players have three counters each. Red and green rice crackers do nicely for us, but any counters that are easily distinguishable, such as bottle tops or coins, will do. Players take turns placing their counters on one of the points on the board. They cannot move their pieces until all three counters have been placed on the board.

If neither player has achieved three in a row after all tokens are on the board, they take turns moving a token along one of the lines from one point to the next, vertically, horizontally, or diagonally, until one player has three in a row. No jumping is allowed. If neither player can make another move, the game is deemed a tie. The game is quite addictive, as you wrack your brains to think of a foolproof way to win.

NINE MEN'S MORRIS

What better way to while away a good half hour or so than with a strategy game whose origins are firmly rooted with the ancients but which, in modern times, could involve peanuts, chocolate freckles, and a bit of playful competition? This is a chance to make and play a homemade board game with a difference.

NUMBER OF PLAYERS	2
AGE	9 and up
YOU WILL NEED	Pen, paper or cardboard, and two different types of counters (9 per player — perhaps buttons, rice crackers, chocolate coins …)
PLAYING TIME	10 minutes per game

OBJECT OF THE GAME
To leave the opposing player with fewer than three counters or with no legal moves available to them.

HOW TO PLAY
On a piece of paper or cardboard, rule up a board, as per the illustration:

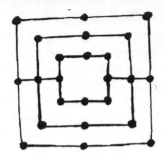

The board has 24 intersections, along which each player can move their nine counters, or 'men'. There are two parts to this game: the 'placing' stage, and the 'playing' stage. At each stage, men can be taken.

Players take it in turns to place each man on an intersection on the board. The goal is for players to form three men in a row, which is called a 'mill'. When they have formed a mill, they can take one man from their opponent from anywhere on the board. However, players can only remove pieces from a formed mill when no other pieces are left to take. The captured piece is put to the side and cannot be placed on the board again. Once all the men have been placed on the board, players take it in turns to move their pieces.

A move is made by sliding your man (vertically or horizontally) across a line to an empty intersection. As in the set-up stage, a player can form a mill and take a piece from his opponent. Once again, he must avoid taking a piece from an opponent's mill, unless there are no other pieces to be had.

Any player who has only two pieces left is not able to remove any of their opponent's pieces, and thus loses. Alternatively, the game is lost if no more legal moves can be made. Cheating by eating the other player's edible counters is expressly forbidden.

It is best at the start of the game to place pieces in versatile locations, rather than trying to quickly form mills. Another good strategy is to form two mills, from which one piece can be shuttled back and forth, leaving the other player in a bit of a spin when their pieces are taken one after another.

The beauty of this game is that the loser can console themselves by eating the other player's chocolate counters. You don't get that in a commercial board game, now, do you?

DID YOU KNOW?

According to R. C. Bell, in *Board and Table Games from Many Civilisations*, one of the earliest mentions of Nine Men's Morris is in Ovid's 'Ars Amatoria', which says that the game is a 'bad thing for a woman not to know how to play, for love often comes into being during play'.

Markings for Nine Men's Morris have been found from ancient Egypt to Rome, and from 1st-century AD Ceylon to Dark Age Scandinavia. The board has also been found carved on the tops of barrels, on ships' timbers, scratched onto flat rocks, and even carved on church pews. Related games are still played today, as far as Ghana, Canton, the Philippines, and China.

While the most common version of the Morris games is Nine Men's Morris, Three Men's Morris, Six Men's Morris, and Twelve Men's Morris are also played.

It can be safely said that this game is well established in the universal collective consciousness of 'games for all time'.

GAMES WITH NUMBERS

Not everything that counts can be counted,
and not everything that can be counted counts.
— Albert Einstein

There are a range of games here to suit all interests and ages, from the mathematically minded to those who shudder at the thought of adding up a simple sum.

Are you feeling lucky? Bingo's your game. A penchant for breaking codes? Try Code-Breaker. Or are you ready to decide your fate? Go for Numerology. Whatever your fancy, roll up, roll up, and place your numbers ...

BINGO

Variously known as Lotto, Tombola, or Housey-Housey, Bingo as we know it today is a direct descendant of the Italian National Lottery, Lo Giuoco del Lotto d'Italia. This lottery has been held at weekly intervals, almost without pause, since 1530. The modern version of the game was popularised by travelling toy-salesman Edward S. Lowe in the late 1920s. He was astounded at the fervour with which it was being played at a local fair, and developed one of the first commercial versions for children.

Bingo is played passionately — some might say obsessively — across the globe, from Bundaberg to Bright, from Edinburgh to Exeter, and from Nevada to New York. God help the poor soul who tries to interrupt a bingo game in progress at the local Senior Citizens' Club — all hell will break loose.

In this game, we don't expect players to be hitting each other with walking sticks: we encourage you to play in the spirit of good old-fashioned fun. Of course, a bit of lively shouting doesn't hurt. So, clickety click, off to it …

PREPARATION

Part of the fun of this game is in making the cards and discs yourself (instructions are available below). You might do this with paper, but card is hardier and you can reuse it. The other fun bit is working out what you will use as 'counters' to cover the numbers once they have been called out. One option is for each player to cut out numbers one to 90 and use these as counters. A more fun option, in our opinion, is to use edible counters, such as chocolate buds. The benefit of these is that you can eat them once you finish the game.

NUMBER OF PLAYERS	2 or more
AGE	4 and up
YOU WILL NEED	Card and paper, 15 small 'counters' per player
PLAYING TIME	15 to 20 minutes per game

OBJECT OF THE GAME

To be the first to complete all the numbers on your game card and call out, 'Bingo!'

HOW TO PLAY

To make the cards, each player draws up a grid of nine rows across and three rows down. On each of the horizontal rows, there should be five numbers across, leaving four blanks at random. On the vertical rows, the numbers in the first column should be any numbers from one to ten; in the second column, any numbers from 11 to 20; in the third column, any numbers from 21 to 30; and so on, as per the example below. This ensures that there is an even spread of random numbers, giving everyone an equal chance of winning. The mathematicians among you will appreciate the reasoning behind this.

5		25	30			61		83
	12			46	55		75	86
	17		36	47	52	68		

You will need the equivalent number of cards to players. You may also choose to make extras, so that there is a range of cards and numbers to choose from when you play the next time.

A grid of numbers from one to 90 should be made up and then cut out, so that you have 90 numbered squares. It helps to underline numerals that may be confused if they are turned upside down: for example, the numbers six and nine.

These are put into a container, and one person is chosen as the 'Bingo master'. The Bingo master pulls out the numbers, one by one, and calls them out. They can add a bit of drama and imagination to the game by creating rhymes, like '36, clickety click', '42 in your moo', '68, it's a race'. If the players have that number, they place a counter where it appears on their card.

The first person to mark off all 15 numbers on their card calls out 'Bingo' and wins the game.

Note: if you want to make the game move along more quickly, you can agree that the first person to finish a row can call out 'bingo'.

VARIATION

In the US version of this game, players have cards with a five by five grid, corresponding to the five letters in the word B-I-N-G-O. This card contains 24 numbered spaces and one blank space in the middle. The numbers in the 'B' column are between one and 15, in the 'I' column between 16 and 30, in the 'N' column (containing four numbers and the free space) between 31 and 45, in the 'G' column between 46 and 60, and in the 'O' column between 61 and 75, as per the example below.

Numbers from one to 75 are then drawn at random out of a possible 75, until one player completes a 'Bingo' pattern, which is a line with five numbers in a vertical, horizontal, or diagonal row.

B	I	N	G	O
2	17	44	47	73
12	27	38	50	65
7	25		54	62
5	30	41	57	71
14	19	32	59	68

TAKING IT TO THE NEXT LEVEL ...
If Bingo takes your fancy, why not host a
Bingo night? Ham it up with blue-rinse
wigs and walking sticks or, better still,
invite a few more senior people in your
life to show you how it's done.

CODE-BREAKER

This game, also known as Bulls and Crows, is known commercially as
Mastermind. The game was invented in the early 1970s by Mordecai
Meirowitz, an Israeli postmaster and telecommunications expert, and went
on to become a commercial hit around the world. Here, we return to the
humble pen-and-paper version of the game.

NUMBER OF PLAYERS	2
AGE	7 and up
YOU WILL NEED	Pen and paper
PLAYING TIME	10 minutes

OBJECT OF THE GAME
To be the first to unscramble the 'code'.

73

HOW TO PLAY

Player 1 must write down a four-digit code using numbers between one and nine: for example: '1, 5, 7, 2'. Suffice to say, their opponent is not allowed to see what their code is.

Player 2 must then make a series of deductive guesses to work out what the code is, by suggesting possible combinations that are written down on a grid, such as the one below. For example, they might suggest '3, 5, 7, 1'. In this instance, the numbers five and seven are right. Player 1 places a tick beside these. She also places a dot by the numbers that are present but not in the right order (in this instance, one). She places a cross next to the numbers that are wrong (in this case, three) so that Player 2 knows not to include that number in their next guess.

A game might proceed as follows:

Player 1 code	1	5	7	2
	3 ✗	5 ✔	7 ✔	1 ●
	1 ✔	5 ✔	7 ✔	4 ✗
Player 2 guesses	1 ✔	5 ✔	7 ✔	6 ✗
	1 ✔	5 ✔	7 ✔	8 ✗
	1 ✔	5 ✔	7 ✔	2 ✔

In this way, Player 2 gets information at each guess that helps him to break the code.

As you get better at this game, you can try duplicating numbers or making the code longer.

VARIATION

You could always play this game with coloured counters (our preference is, as always, for counters of the edible variety, preferably chocolate, of which you will need four different colours or shapes).

NUMEROLOGY

This game has nothing to do with using numbers to tell you about yourself; except, perhaps, to show how competitive players can get. This strangely addictive game is great for a bit of light-hearted post-dinner-party numerical and literary play.

NUMBER OF PLAYERS	2 or more
AGE	8 and up
YOU WILL NEED	Pen and paper, calculator (or brain power, if you prefer)
PLAYING TIME	5 minutes per word or phrase

OBJECT OF THE GAME

To get the highest score by using 'high value' letters.

HOW TO PLAY

To begin, each player needs a sheet of paper. On this, they write the alphabet and attribute a number from one to 26 to each letter, in sequence, so that the letter 'a' equals one, all the way through to 'z', which equals 26.

Players now take it in turns to call out categories (movie titles, animals, kitchen implements), and each player has to write down a word or phrase within that category. Each player then calculates the numerical value of their word (for example, the word 'zebra' would be calculated as follows: 26 + 5 + 2 + 18 + 1 = 52 points).

After each round, players' scores are recorded on a score sheet. The player who earns the most points wins.

26 + 5 + 2 + 18 + 1 = 52 POINTS

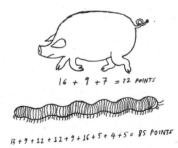

16 + 9 + 7 = 32 POINTS

13 + 9 + 12 + 12 + 9 + 16 + 5 + 4 + 5 = 85 POINTS

THE SHOW MUST GO ON!

GAMES OF MOTION, MYSTERY, AND MAKE-BELIEVE

These here are the 'doing' games, the 'verbs' of the book. You can forget the thoughtful wordplay, the lazy shuffle of the cards; most of these games require your getting up off the chair, or floor, and joining in the action. For some, you are going to end up looking very silly. There is not much point-scoring in this section: the point is simply to have fun.

There are some old favourites here, such as Charades, Wink Murder, and Blind Man's Buff, and others that are likely to take you by surprise — in a good way. The Sock Game, for example, has been a minor revelation to us. Some of the games are unruly, but all fit comfortably indoors.

One group of games is based upon the premise of trying to keep a straight face while doing something daft, but we defy you not to laugh through most of the games in this section; and laughter, along with beetroot juice, is very good for your health (see p. 128).

GAMES WITH BLINDFOLDS

You tie a scarf over your eyes, to remove your sight, and then stagger about the room dangerously unbalanced, disoriented, vulnerable, and absurd. And you do this voluntarily — for fun! In fact, people have been doing this kind of thing for a couple of thousand years. A version of Blind Man's Buff was being played in Greece at the time of the Roman Conquest.

Blindfolds, from Middle English *blindfellen*, are employed in many parlour games and, as well as being thrilling (and hilarious), they draw our attention in an interesting way to the other senses. We have to understand the world through what we feel, hear, smell, and taste. We get to notice the deep timbre of Dad's voice, or the cool smoothness of an egg.

It is sensible when playing the more active blindfold games to take some basic safety precautions. Clear everything off the floor. Where possible, play in an area large enough to allow plenty of dodging, and where there aren't too many sharp corners. In our houses, sighted players have to stay within a designated area of the open-plan living space to give the Blind Man a sporting chance.

For a blindfold, use a light scarf, a strip of sheeting, a sleep mask from an aeroplane trip, or a beanie, pulled down over the eyes. Obviously, the blindfold has to be well fitted but not so as to cut off circulation. And, of course, no peeking.

BLINDFOLDED AIM

This is the parlour game from which Pin the Tail on the Donkey was derived. You can draw or cut out pictures to pin something onto, or you can play this game simply using your finger and a mark on the wall.

NUMBER OF PLAYERS	2 to 10
AGE	3 and up
YOU WILL NEED	A blindfold, a mark on a wall, and a ruler (donkeys and tails, etc., optional)
PLAYING TIME	10 minutes

OBJECT OF THE GAME

To get the closest to touching a mark on the wall when blindfolded.

HOW TO PLAY

Locate a spot already on a wall: an old smear of spaghetti sauce is good, or sometimes we use the nose of a funny character on a child's drawing that is stuck at just the right height on the laundry door. If your walls are so clean that you can't find a mark to use, make one with pencil or chalk.

Position the first player behind a starting line (for example, the edge of a rug), about two to three metres away from the wall. Once in position, the player is blindfolded and must now attempt to walk to the wall and use her finger to touch the spot. No groping or feeling around for corners or other landmarks is permitted. When the player's finger touches the wall, they must keep it there without moving until the blindfold is removed and a ruler is used to measure the distance from their finger to the spot. Despite *feeling* that they've walked in a straight line, players will usually find they've swerved a little and, for some reason, fingers often end up a little higher than their intended destination.

One after the other, each of the players is blindfolded and has their go at getting as close as they can to the spot. When everyone has had a turn, whoever's blindfolded aim was the best wins! Sometimes, we play a match and have three goes each, and our cumulative scores are added to find a winner. It is amazing how much your aim improves on second and third tries.

VARIATION

If you want to be more elaborate, you can pin up a picture of a donkey, make a separate tail, and have players try to pin the tail onto the donkey's behind (Blu-Tack is somewhat safer, and easier on the wall, than a drawing pin). Or, as we have done in the past, draw a web with a fly on it, and try to stick a rubber spider onto the fly. If it's a birthday party, stick a nose on a drawing of the birthday boy's face ... Or, if it's a housewarming, put a chimney on a picture of your new home.

MAD SCIENTIST

This is a wonderful sensory-detective game that is fun for players of all ages. With older kids and adults, you can start introducing weirder ingredients: cinnamon, smoked oysters, wasabi peas, durian, anyone? It goes without saying that you will need to check first if any players have food allergies and tailor the game accordingly.

NUMBER OF PLAYERS	3 to 8
AGE	3 and up
YOU WILL NEED	A selection of foodstuffs, a tray, paper and pen for scoring, and a blindfold for each player
PLAYING TIME	20 minutes

OBJECT OF THE GAME

To be the fastest at correctly identifying the most foodstuffs.

HOW TO PLAY

One or two players volunteer for the job of Mad Scientist. For four or fewer players, one scientist will generally suffice; for any more, you will need at least two scientists to administer test samples to the blindfolded subjects.

Players are sent out of the room, while the scientists gather food samples together on the tray. There should be at least six but up to 20 foodstuffs cut into small pieces, or ready on teaspoons, in portions equal to the number of blindfolded players. For younger kids, try lemon, carrot, dried apricot, cheese, cracker, cold cooked rice, liquorice, or whatever else you can find in your pantry. For older kids, go all out and get obscure with flavours and textures. Our kids have been stumped by tiny slivers of raw garlic, pine nuts, and baby capers! Maybe give the chilli paste a miss.

All the players, apart from the Mad Scientist, are blindfolded and sit up at a bench or table in the kitchen laboratory. At the command 'open', all the players open their mouths, and a small piece of food is quickly popped into each one. You want samples to be administered simultaneously, if possible, hence the need for more than one scientist if you have several subjects. The first player to correctly identify the food wins that round and gets one point.

Continue until all the foods have been sampled. The player with the most points at the end of the game wins. If there is a tie, only the players who have tied can do one last bonus tasting. Pick something really obscure to see who takes the prize for most sensitive taster.

VARIATIONS

This game is equally fun when subjects are given things to smell rather than to taste; in this case, you are not limited to food. Add soap, gum leaves, soil from the garden, Dad's sneaker, etc.

We also play Mad Scientist with a feeling tray, where the blindfolded player is given household objects to feel: a hairbrush, an egg, a can opener, a cork … Experiment with anything that comes to hand, but look for objects that are going to be hard to get a handle on.

In the above two variations, you are unlikely to have multiple samples for your subjects, so you can either test blindfolded players one at a time or, as we do, just play for fun.

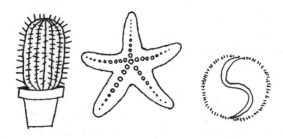

BLIND MAN'S BUFF

Blind Man's Buff is the archetypal blindfold parlour game. It still makes an appearance at children's birthday parties, but our families have also played it at home after dinner and had a ball! It is very funny to watch someone you love staggering around blindfolded, waving their arms uselessly as they are poked and tickled; but it's also a strange and wonderful experience taking your turn behind the blindfold. In Italy, this game is known as *Mosca Cieca*, which means 'blind fly'. In France, it is called *Colin-Maillard*, after a medieval battle in which a poor fellow, Jean Colin-Maillard, continued to fight on after being blinded.

NUMBER OF PLAYERS	4 to 15
AGE	5 and up
YOU WILL NEED	A bunch of willing participants, a large-ish space to play in, and a blindfold
PLAYING TIME	20 minutes

OBJECT OF THE GAME

To catch one of the other players when blindfolded and identify them correctly by touch.

HOW TO PLAY

One player volunteers, or is chosen, to go first. This player is then blindfolded and spun around several times on the spot, so as to lose his bearings. Completely disoriented, the Blind Man now has to move around the room with arms outstretched like a zombie, trying to catch one of the other players.

A large part of the fun is in the other players taunting and making daring moves towards him; gentle prodding, tickling, or tugging of clothes is OK. At one time, the game was played a little more roughly: the Blind Man was pushed and sometimes struck, hence 'buff', which is Middle English for 'blow'. But people didn't get sued back then.

When the Blind Man finally manages to capture another player, he has to identify the person by touch. This is easy if there are only a few of you playing, and if some are much shorter or hairier than others. If there are lots of players, a good feel of the face is the way to go. Only if the person is correctly identified does the Blind Man get to relinquish the blindfold and the prisoner take his place.

VARIATION

Play Blind Man's Buff in reverse. All players except one are blindfolded, and all are trying to catch hold of the one sighted player, who has to dodge in and out, verbally taunting and touching the Blind Men. The Blind Men will keep grabbing hold of one another, instead of their intended prey. When the sighted player is eventually seized, he has to swap places with his captor and the game starts again. (This variation is known as The Bellman if the sighted player wanders around ringing a bell.)

ALL IN A SPIN

In Victorian England, there was a rhyme that sometimes accompanied the spinning of the blindfolded player. The Blind Man was asked by another player: 'How many horses has your father got?' to which he would answer, 'Three.'

He was then asked: 'What colour are they?' to which he replied, 'Black, white, and grey.'

The questioner finished by saying, as he spun him around: 'Turn around three times, and catch who you may!'

SQUEAK, PIGGY, SQUEAK

This is another variation on the Blind Man theme but, this time, you have to rely on your sense of hearing, rather than touch, to work out whose lap you have landed on. It's another game guaranteed to get you giggling as players try hard to disguise their snorts and oinks. This is a good one for a party or larger group; if there are only a few of you, it can be too easy to identify the piggy.

NUMBER OF PLAYERS	6 to 15
AGE	5 and up
YOU WILL NEED	A blindfold and a cushion
PLAYING TIME	10 minutes

OBJECT OF THE GAME

To sit on one of the other players' laps when blindfolded and identify them correctly by voice.

HOW TO PLAY

Everyone has to sit in a circle for this one, either on chairs or on the floor, apart from one player, who is blindfolded and put in the middle of the circle. Holding a cushion, the Blind Man has to spin around three times, so as to lose her bearings. She then totters about until she makes physical contact with one of the other players. She promptly puts the cushion on this person's lap and sits down. The Blind Man is not otherwise allowed to touch the seated player or his clothing. While the Blind Man can mutter all she likes, all other players should remain completely silent to avoid detection.

Once seated, the Blind Man commands, 'Squeak, Piggy, Squeak!' The person whose lap she is on then has to make a squeaky, piggy noise, and the Blind Man has to try to guess who it is. If she correctly identifies the voice, the Blind Man and the Piggy swap places, and the game starts over. However, if she guesses incorrectly, the Blind Man goes back into the middle and is spun around again before looking for another lap. While the Blind Man is being spun around, other players can swap places to make things more confusing.

VARIATION

Animals is another great Blind Man game involving voice identification, and it's a better game when you have fewer players. Players wander freely around the room, getting as close as they dare to the Blind Man, as in Blind Man's Buff, until one is captured. When captured, this player has to make an animal noise — donkey, cat, rooster, whatever — on the basis of which the Blind Man has to guess their identity. If correct, they swap places; if incorrect, the captive is let go, and the Blind Man sets out to catch another beastie.

BURGLARS

It's hard enough negotiating obstacles when you can see, but try doing it blindfolded, like a burglar in the dark. It's a lot of fun. Kids enjoy setting up the obstacle course almost as much as playing on it. This is a great one for parties.

NUMBER OF PLAYERS	3 to 15
AGE	5 and up
YOU WILL NEED	Whatever large and small obstacles you can gather together to make a course, a blindfold, and a stopwatch (optional)
PLAYING TIME	30 minutes

OBJECT OF THE GAME
To get to the end of the obstacle course in the fastest time, or simply to get there in one piece.

HOW TO PLAY
First, you have to create an obstacle course, making it as easy or hard as you like, depending on the ages of those playing. You don't want any broken limbs.

Here are some ideas: have the course start with a blind music recital: piano, drums, or whatever instrument you have to hand. For the course itself, use boxes to step over; a row of chairs to crawl along; a card table to crawl under; lengths of string tied at different levels, to either go over or under; buckets of water to dodge; a step ladder to scale, etc. Finish the course with a dish of chocolate frogs. Use your imagination — setting up the course is part of the fun.

Once the course has been constructed, everyone gets to go through once or twice without blindfolds, before the first player steps up for the real challenge. She is blindfolded, and at 'Go!' she has to negotiate her way from one end of the course to the other. A timekeeper can record start and finish times, or you can just play for fun. Other players keep a watch on the contestant's progress to keep her safe, and they can help her out verbally when need be.

Each player gets a turn to blindly navigate the course and, if you want to play competitively, the person with the fastest time is the winner. Hopefully, this won't encourage them into a life of crime.

THE BLINDFOLDED HOUSE TOUR

For a fantastic sensory experience, blindfold one player and take them on a tour of their own home. Disorientate them by doing lots of loop-the-loops and walking them backwards and forwards until they have no idea where they are. Then, let them start feeling their way around, experiencing their own stuff without sight. See how long it takes for them to work out what room they are in, and then take them by the hand and mess with their heads again by looping the loop before continuing the tour again.

THE SOCK GAME

Ever wanted to be a gladiator? Two blindfolded players have to try to hit each other with socks while a bloodthirsty audience looks on. Beautiful! This will leave you breathless and elated.

NUMBER OF PLAYERS	4, plus audience
AGE	7 and up
YOU WILL NEED	Two pairs of balled-up socks and two blindfolds
PLAYING TIME	15 minutes

OBJECT OF THE GAME

To be the first blindfolded player to hit the other blindfolded player.

HOW TO PLAY

There are only two contestants in any one round, with a retriever for each, so four people can play this game; but there can be an unlimited audience.

The two contestants are blindfolded and guided by their personal retrievers to opposite ends of the room. They are each given a pair of balled-up socks and then spun around three times to disorient them. At 'Let the battle begin ...', each player has to throw the sock in the direction in which they think the other player is, in the hope of hitting them. Generally, it doesn't happen on the first attempt.

The job of the retrievers is to pick up the nearest pair of tossed socks and hand them to the contestants so they can keep playing. Apart from putting socks in hands, neither the retrievers nor the audience are allowed to touch the contestants or tell them where the other contestant is; but they can cheer and barrack, and say, 'That was close,' all of which helps the contestants' job.

For their part, the blindfolded contestants have to rely on their hearing, audience feedback, and their intuitive sense to decide where to throw. They throw every time they get the socks in their hands, until one succeeds in hitting the other and is declared the winner!

Contestants now swap positions with retrievers, and the game starts over. Depending on how many players you have, set up a tournament and conduct play-offs until you have an ultimate sock-wielding champion.

BLIND POTATOES

Another fabulous game, and one of our family favourites. The world seems a superb place when you get to race blindfolded across the floor, on hands and knees, picking up potatoes. Bring it on.

NUMBER OF PLAYERS	3 to 10
AGE	7 and up
YOU WILL NEED	20 to 30 potatoes (or onions, or oranges, or balls, or just about any other unbreakable object of similar size); a blindfold for each racer; and an hourglass, a stopwatch, or clock
PLAYING TIME	5 minutes

OBJECT OF THE GAME
To retrieve the most potatoes from the floor.

HOW TO PLAY
Depending on how many players you have, you can split into teams and play a couple of rounds, or just have two or three of you racing against one another. You need at least one sighted player to scatter potatoes. Whether working solo or representing a partnership or team, you don't want more than three or four blindfolded players on the floor at any one time.

Once the racers' sight has been disabled and they've been left at the starting line — for example, the edge of the rug — another player has to scatter potatoes all over the floor. At 'Go!', the racers crawl out, and they have exactly one minute to collect as many potatoes as they can, wedging them under arms, in the folds of a baggy top, in pockets, or anywhere else. Some of our kids have worked out that stuffing them down their pants works best. The sighted players looking on may need to referee and make the call on who got there first, if any blind potato-related squabbles start up.

When called to stop, after the minute is up, racers remove blindfolds, and the racer with the most potatoes wins the round. Note: you will probably need to vacuum up potato dirt.

VARIATION

If you want to play a trick on the racers, you can pretend to scatter potatoes — make sure you include sound effects. Cry 'Go!' and watch players race all over the rug, grabbing at nothing. Film it and keep it for a 21st.

BERNIE DEKOVEN ON THE 'PLAYFUL PATH' AND 'DEEP FUN'

Bernie DeKoven, Indianapolis-based author of *The Well-Played Game: a playful path to wholeness* and *Junkyard Sports*, has spent the past 45 years studying and teaching the art and science of play.

As well as writing about games, Bernie has developed a five-volume games curriculum for elementary schools in Philadelphia. He designs card games and computer games, and he has worked with the international movement the New Games Foundation to introduce a non-competitive games model into communities throughout the world. Bernie also runs regular training programs and retreats for adults to help them embrace the 'Playful Path' and experience the transformative power of 'Deep Fun'. The self-declared 'funsmith' spoke with us about the serious work of playing games:

> I was the child who frequently wound up in the principal's office. I kept on cracking jokes; they tried to impress seriousness upon me, but they were not that successful. I remember distinctly, early on in elementary school, being just so surprised that workbooks and homework and the things teachers were making us do were *not fun*. I really believed things should be a lot more fun than they had turned out to be. It was from this point, I guess, that I began to devote myself to what I call the 'Playful Path'.
>
> In high school, I discovered theatre, and there was a lot of playfulness in theatre. Improvisation was playful. So, when I graduated, I started teaching at elementary school by day, taking a master's degree in theatre by night, and I was invited to develop a curriculum in children's theatre for schools in

Philadelphia. I wanted to find a form of theatre that was native to children, not something imposed upon them, and this led me back to games. I discovered that children's games *are* a form of theatre. I began to appreciate them as a whole dramaturgy — very complex, very profound, and very revealing about the nature of life and the child's perspective of reality. Even the simplest games have this tremendous amount of drama that goes on in them. So, I wound up writing a curriculum of children's games, instead of a curriculum of theatre. It involved five volumes and a thousand games, and it looked at games as a real subject to be explored. When I started teaching teachers how to use this curriculum, I discovered that adults needed the opportunity to play with each other just as much as children did.

In order to go more deeply into the study of fun, I bought a 25-acre farm in north-eastern Pennsylvania, and converted the big barn into the ultimate playroom. I called it the 'Games Preserve'. I held workshops there, helping adults to explore the nature of games and playfulness.

It was at the Games Preserve that I really began to appreciate the power of play. We had sessions in exploring playfulness that were really, really profound, that were as spiritual and as joyous as you could imagine. I made two life-changing discoveries: the first, that fun is fundamental to happiness; the second, that people can learn how to have more fun. I also noticed that the less fun people were having, the more alienated they felt.

Trying to make yourself happy is like trying to tickle yourself: you can tickle yourself, but you're not going to laugh. You have to have somebody else tickle you; which is, I guess, why I like games that involve playing with other people. I don't think you can really make yourself happy, but you *can* choose to have fun. You can choose to be playful, and that's what the Playful Path is about. I call it a 'path' because it applies to everything that you do and think and believe; it extends from home to the workplace, from family out into society at large. Playfulness becomes a way of life that leads, ultimately, to wholeness.

The best way that I've found to teach playfulness is through 'Deep Fun', a method that combines 'pointless' games with deep reflection. I call them 'pointless' for a couple of reasons, not the least of which is that, in most of them, you don't keep score; and, in the rest, the score doesn't really matter. When you're playing games that you know are pointless, you escape that whole aspect of ego that gets involved in a lot of our traditional games and sports. Once you really embrace pointless play, you begin to open up to yourself, to the people that you're with, to the environment that you're in; you become childlike, in the best sense. Because pointless games don't *mean* anything, you can't attach anything to them; they are too funny to be taken seriously, so you begin to acknowledge the sheer power of being at play.

When Hungarian professor Mihaly Csikszentmihalyi was creating his Flow Theory, he talked with people who go hang-gliding and rock-climbing, people going to extreme lengths to have fun. When you're at that level, it's a very deep kind of fun. You are fully engaged, your body is engaged, your senses, your mind, and your spirit. All that inner dialogue that says 'I'm not good enough,' or 'That's not good enough for me,' disappears. You feel a 'oneness' with yourself and the environment and the people you're sharing the experience with.

You feel this same thing, this *Deep Fun*, when you're playing a pointless game. When you're playing a game with other people, you're creating fun together; you are empowering that experience, and that experience is empowering you, so the fun you're having reaches deeper, the laughter is more profound, you laugh with your entire body. You experience a sense of exhilaration and timelessness, of perfect focus.

It's important always to remember that the game does not matter as much as the fun you're experiencing with each other. It's not the game itself but the playful contract between people that matters.

I think the world is as fun as it always has been. I think what's changed is that there's less acceptance of people having fun in any kind of public environment. If you're laughing, people start looking at you as if you are either crazy or definitely not doing what you're supposed to be doing. Playfulness is suspect. I don't think it was that way 100 years ago. Those people who do those bizarre things where they go into a train station and all start dancing ... people like that are helping us all to become the kind of free people we're supposed to be.

GAMES OF HIDE AND SEEK

A great thinker of our time, Jean Baudrillard, mused:

> One of life's primal situations; the game of hide and seek. Oh, the delicious thrill of hiding while the others come looking for you, the delicious terror of being discovered, but what panic when, after a long search, the others abandon you! You mustn't hide too well. You mustn't be too good at the game. The player must never be bigger than the game itself.

He captures perfectly the double-edged thrill of hiding in the back of the musty coat cupboard while your friend thumps flat-footed across the floorboards outside, just metres away. (By the way, this thrill is by no means limited to children. Try playing Hide and Seek at an adult dinner party.) You don't want to be found, but then you also do. You would just like to be found *last*, and then delivered from that lonely, claustrophobic, primal place.

While hiding may be thrilling, seeking seems to satisfy another basic human instinct, whether we are looking for friends, objects in a treasure hunt, recurring motifs in a picture book, or a slippery ring on a string. We all love to find what we are looking for. *There it is! I found it!* We love to be good at this. Maybe it's our hunter-gatherer beginnings, where one's very survival depended upon our wits and a pair of sharp eyes.

So, put the blindfold away now, and summon your inner caveman. These games are guaranteed to satisfy your deepest hide-and-seek urges.

HOT BUTTERED BEANS

In Hot Buttered Beans, it's not a person but an object that is hidden and sought. This is an especially good one for small children who love the concept of getting 'hotter' and 'colder' as they move towards and away from the hidden object.

NUMBER OF PLAYERS	2 to 6
AGE	3 and up
YOU WILL NEED	Any small object, and a room with adequate clutter
PLAYING TIME	10 minutes

OBJECT OF THE GAME
To find the hidden object as quickly as possible.

HOW TO PLAY
First, players agree on a small object to hide. This can be anything: an action figure, a walnut, a bottle of nail varnish. One player is sent out of the room (either a volunteer or the loser of a quick round of Scissors, Paper, Stone, p. 143), while the others find a really good hiding place for the object. Once they've hidden it, the players call out: 'Hot buttered beans! Please come to supper!'

At this, the exiled player returns and starts to search for the missing object. Throughout, the other players help, by informing the seeker if he is getting 'cold', 'very cold', 'icy', or 'warm', 'warmer', 'hot', 'burning', according to how close or far the seeker is to the object.

Once the object has been found, it is another player's turn to be sent out, until all the players have had the opportunity to be seeker.

There are no winners or losers in this game.

HUNT THE THIMBLE

Also known as Hide in Sight, this is a great variation of Hot Buttered Beans, because the object is 'hidden' in plain view. It's like a 3D version of an I-Spy book. How long will it take for you to spot the thimble?

NUMBER OF PLAYERS	2 to 10
AGE	3 and up
YOU WILL NEED	A thimble (or other small object) and a cluttered room
PLAYING TIME	10 minutes

OBJECT OF THE GAME

To be the first player to find the thimble, or to not be the last to find it.

HOW TO PLAY

In 19th-century parlours, thimbles were easy to come by. If you don't have one in your sewing chest (or if you don't even have a sewing chest), then any small article will suffice. We sometimes use a tiny plastic Indian who blends beautifully with the books on the shelf.

All players but one must leave the room this time. The hider then chooses a conspicuous yet camouflaged position to place the object (putting it by something of the same colour is a good start). It has to be clearly visible without anything needing to be moved aside.

When the seekers are called back in, the hider sits down and the hunt begins. When they find the object, however, the seekers are not to touch it or make any kind of remark; instead, they are to sit down silently on a chair or on the floor (but not right beside the object). Before sitting down, it's good to pretend to keep looking for a bit to throw others off the scent; and, once sitting, it is important not to stare at the object.

This continues until there is just one player left hunting, usually the target of some gentle jibes. When all the seekers have found the thimble, the one who first spotted it gets to hide it next time round.

VARIATION

Play a real-life game of Spot the Difference. All players bar one go outside, while the player that remains makes five changes around the room. They should swap some ornaments around, take a picture off the wall, fiddle with the hands on the clock, that kind of thing. When the players come back, they have to try to spot what's different without saying anything aloud. The first person to find the five differences pipes up. If correct, he is the winner for that round and then gets to make the adjustments for the next. If incorrect, he is out of the game and someone else volunteers their five differences. If no one spots all the differences, the same player gets to do the messing around again.

HIDE AND SEEK

Also known as Hidey, this is another game that has been played for literally thousands of years, sprouting numerous variations and thrilling countless children and adults alike. Here is the classic version that most of us played as kids.

NUMBER OF PLAYERS	4 to 20
AGE	4 and up
YOU WILL NEED	Willing players, and a house with plenty of good hidey-holes
PLAYING TIME	15 minutes

OBJECT OF THE GAME

To be the last person found by the seeker; or, if you are the seeker, to find all the hidden players.

HOW TO PLAY

Choose a 'home base' where everyone gathers — say, the kitchen or bathroom — and then select the first seeker. This person has to cover his eyes and count to 50, slowly and in a loud voice, while everyone else scatters and hides throughout the house. If you want to, you can specify rooms that are off limits.

At the count of 50, the seeker calls out, 'Ready or not, here I come!' and sets off in search of the other players. When they have each been found, they return to home base. The seeker for the next round is then the player whose hiding place was discovered first. If, however, the seeker is unable to find all of the players, he can call out to indicate that he has given up. Players then leave their hiding places, and the same seeker has to try again in the next round.

VARIATIONS

You can make the classic game more active by adding a racing element. Instead of simply finding the hiders, when the seeker discovers a player, they have to tag them and then race them back to home base.

If the seeker gets there first, the player is considered caught; if the hider gets to home base first, she cries, 'Home free!' and, though found, she has not been caught.

Players who are hiding can also make a dash to home base *before* they are found, so the seeker must always keep an eye on what is happening around home base as well as searching out hidden players. The first player 'caught' is seeker in the next round.

Hares and Hounds is another great Victorian variant of Hide and Seek, and a good one for larger groups or parties. The game starts with two seekers, the hounds, who have to sniff out the rest of the players, the hares. When a hound finds a hare, they tap them three times on the shoulder to turn them into a hound (traditionally, this transformation involved three sharp claps to the head). These new hounds join the hunting party, so that, by the end of the game, a whole bunch of hounds will be hunting for the last hare. This makes for an increasingly fast and furious game.

ONE CHIMPANZEE, TWO CHIMPANZEES ...

To make sure the seeker doesn't count too fast while the other players are finding their hiding places, it is traditional to add a little special something to the counting to stretch it out. Common variations are 'one Mississippi, two Mississippi ...', or 'one chimpanzee, two chimpanzees'. 'Elephants' and 'cats and dogs' get a look in, too. Make up your own. (Personally, we like to put some 'spaghetti' in there.)

Adding the extra words mean you should get roughly a second out of each number, and players should be well hidden by the time the seeker sets off.

SARDINES

This is an especially fun and silly back-to-front variation of Hide and Seek. Children and adults alike have to work hard in this game to muffle their laughter, or their communal cover will be blown, revealing all the squishy little fishies therein.

NUMBER OF PLAYERS	4 to 20
AGE	4 and up
YOU WILL NEED	As above: willing (and supple) players, and good (and spacious) hidey-holes
PLAYING TIME	10 minutes

OBJECT OF THE GAME
To not be the last seeker to find the hiders.

HOW TO PLAY
This game begins like classic Hide and Seek, but in reverse. All players except one cover their eyes and count slowly to 50, while one chosen player runs off to

hide. When finished, they all shout out, 'Ready or not, here we come,' and set off in search of the hidden player. For the game to work, the seekers have to spread out across the house and not stay bunched up as a group.

When one of the seekers finds the hider, she waits until there is no one else looking — moving on and then doubling back, if necessary — and then creeps into the hiding place, too. (Obviously, the hider has to choose a spot that can accommodate a few players, but part of the fun is to be squashed in, like sardines in a tin.)

As the seekers slowly disappear, the hiding spot becomes increasingly squashy, until the very last seeker comes upon all the sardines, thereby bringing the game to an end. This last seeker then has to hide first in the next round.

VARIATION
To make Sardines even more thrilling, play it at night in total or semi-darkness. (Another one for adult dinner parties?)

THE MEMORY TRAY

It was a bit tricky working out where to put this wonderful memory game, but we decided it was a game of Hide and Seek: after studying a tray full of objects, these objects are hidden, and players have to seek, in the recesses of their brains, to remember what on earth they were. It is also known as Kim's Game, because the main character played it during his spy training in Rudyard Kipling's 1901 novel, *Kim*. Fun and competitive, the Memory Tray is also a great exercise in observation and recall.

NUMBER OF PLAYERS	2 to 6
AGE	5 and up
YOU WILL NEED	A tray, a cloth, between 10 and 20 small objects, paper and pen, and a stopwatch
PLAYING TIME	10 minutes

OBJECT OF THE GAME
To remember as many of the objects as you can.

HOW TO PLAY
One player is nominated the conductor, and he gathers together between ten and 20 small household objects and places them on a tray. Absolutely anything will do: a pencil, an orange, a paperclip, a mobile phone, a pair of spectacles, etc. He should adapt the number of articles to suit the ages of the players, and increase it as they get better at the game.

Players are then given one minute to study and memorise the items, before the tray is covered with a cloth. They are then given two minutes to write down as many items as they can remember from the tray.

Players submit their lists, after which they can look again at the Memory Tray to see what they got wrong and right. For each item remembered correctly, one point is scored. However, if a player writes down an item that was never there, they lose a point.

The conductor then conceals the tray again and secretly removes a single item. When he brings it back, players study the tray, and the first person to work out what is missing wins three bonus points.

TREASURE AND SCAVENGER HUNTS

Everyone loves a treasure hunt with clues, or a scavenger hunt where you have to search for particular items. There are no real rules for these hunts; just make them up to suit what you have to hand, the ages and number of players, and the occasion. Below are a few ideas to help get you started.

NUMBER OF PLAYERS	2 to 20
AGE	4 and up
YOU WILL NEED	Treasures/objects to hunt (anything from an old shoe to a cache of chocolate coins), paper and pens to make clues (optional)
PLAYING TIME	10 to 60 minutes

OBJECT OF THE GAME

To find all the treasure or objects, and/or to get to the end of the hunt first.

HOW TO PLAY

You can set up a hunt any old way you like. For a simple scavenger hunt, dispense with written clues and give players ten minutes to find ten objects around the house that are coloured red, or that remind them of summer, or of their Uncle Ted. Or make a list of ten particular items to hunt for. Or send players out of the room and hide sweets (or nuts in their shells) in tricky places. Call them back in and let the hunt begin, adding spoils to one central pool, and dividing it up evenly at the end.

For a treasure hunt, choose around ten locations, and make a handwritten clue to hide in each that will lead seekers to the next. For example, the first clue, handed to players, might be: 'I am the last thing you do before bed, I have a very bristly head,' leading seekers to the bathroom, where a clue is tucked in with the toothbrushes. You can include small treasures at locations along the way, or save them all for the booty at the end of the hunt. For very young children, clues can be pictures rather than words.

It's fun for players to work together on a treasure hunt, and if you have heaps of seekers, they can be divided into teams. At each location, have separate clues in envelopes marked for each team, and arrange it so that they move through the series of locations in different orders. First team to the end wins.

Finally, consider giving the treasure hunt a theme. For a children's birthday party with a pirate theme, for example, burn the edges of handwritten clues and write elaborate swashbuckling rhymes. At the end, have a big sugary booty of choc-chip cookies. For a 21st, hide 21 clues.

I AM THE LAST THING YOU DO BEFORE BED,
I HAVE A VERY BRISTLY HEAD.

WHERE IS THE SQUEEZE?

This is a fun circle game — another great one for parties or family holidays.

Tip: to work out where the squeeze is, watch players' faces as well as their hands.

NUMBER OF PLAYERS	6 to 20
AGE	5 and up
YOU WILL NEED	A bunch of players
PLAYING TIME	10 minutes

OBJECT OF THE GAME
If you are the seeker, to work out where the squeeze is; if you are the hider, to hide it from the seeker.

HOW TO PLAY
Players stand in a circle holding hands, while the seeker stands alone in the middle. The seeker closes his eyes for the count of ten, while one of the

hiders starts up the squeeze. The squeeze is passed between players' hands but can only ever be in one place at one time — no extra squeezes!

The seeker now opens his eyes and has to look around the circle, trying to find where the squeeze is. Hiders should be as surreptitious as they can with the squeeze, taking advantage of moments when the seeker's back is turned, but they are not allowed to hold on to the squeeze for more than ten seconds.

When the seeker correctly locates the squeeze, he gets to swap places with the hider, and the game starts over.

VARIATION

Ring on a String is a lovely Victorian parlour game for a large group that involves hiding a ring on a length of string. Thread the ring onto the string, then cut it and tie it up, so that the loop formed is the same size as your circle of players. Voila: Ring on a String! All bar one player take hold of the string. The odd one out stands in the middle with eyes closed, while the hiders begin moving the ring along the string, keeping it concealed beneath their hands. After a count of ten, the seeker opens his eyes and has to work out who is hiding the ring. The hiders try to fool him with plenty of staged movements, while the ring moves back and forth around the circle in any direction. When the middle man guesses correctly who has the ring in their fist, he swaps places with this player, and hider becomes seeker.

FOR THE LOVE OF FORFEITS

In parlours of old, if a player was penalised for a misdemeanour during a game — if they got an answer wrong, or they took too long on their turn — they would have to offer up one of their personal belongings (a hat or brooch, say) to be held by the forfeit-master until the end of the evening.

After the games were over, players would have to perform forfeits (tasks designed to make them look brilliant or silly, basically) in order to get their possessions back. This was often the most madcap part of the evening.

With time, the business of confiscating and returning items was considered too onerous, and forfeits were written up on bits of paper and handed out to penalised players. In Throwing the Smile (p. 127), for example, the first player to smile out of turn would have been given a forfeit.

The tradition of giving and redeeming forfeits in game playing has all but disappeared; we are more focused these days on rewards (of sweets and small plastic toys). However, if making your fellow-players work off their failures in humiliating ways holds appeal, there are some great forfeits you can bring into your play. Play a game of Taboo (p. 263) or Sly Simon Says (p. 147), for example, and have the person who goes out first perform a forfeit.

These days, forfeits are commonly played as games in themselves. Write a whole lot of them, including some long, tricky ones, on little bits of paper, and put them into a hat. Spin a bottle, draw cards, or roll dice to see who dips in first. Make a night of it.

Below are some old and some modern forfeits to get you started. If you like the sound of these, you'll soon appreciate that this is an area in which you can get very creative.

- Get into the starting position for a race and sing the national anthem in falsetto
- Collect, within three minutes, six objects beginning with the letter p
- Exchange shoes and socks with the person to your right
- Name five movies starring Julia Roberts
- Impersonate a lizard
- Compose and sing a song about pickled eggs
- Whistle 'Waltzing Matilda' without laughing or smiling
- Stand on your hands with your feet against the wall
- Be spoon-fed ice-cream by the person on your left
- Recite a poem
- Touch all four corners of the room within ten seconds
- Name all the continents and oceans of the world
- Spell 'palaeontologist'
- Kiss the feet of everyone playing
- Confess your greatest sin
- Name five animals beginning with the letter k

- Put on a blindfold and apply lipstick to the nearest fella
- Name six planets
- Tell a joke
- Name five songs with 'love' in the title
- Go around the room and give each player a piece of advice
- Say the alphabet backwards while touching your toes

And so on. You might also think on a grander scale, as in this group forfeit from Patrick Beaver's *Victorian Parlour Games*:

> *Blind Dancers*: If the end of the party is nigh and there are still many forfeits to be redeemed, those left to do penance may all be blindfolded and compelled to go through the motions of whatever is the popular dance of the day. This collective punishment (which sometimes threatens to become a massacre) makes a good finale to any party.

Ah, the pleasure.

GAMES OF MAKE-BELIEVE

All of us, children and adults alike, make-believe on a regular basis, often without realising it. It is our ability to make-believe — perhaps in a delicious daydream over lunch — that feeds our creativity. Whether we are designing a new garden, writing a play, painting a picture, or dreaming up new combinations for dinner, it is enriching and productive to imagine your way into something or someone else.

More importantly, for our current purposes, it's fun. The games in this section, from the timeless Charades to the exciting Murder in the Dark and the hilarious Adverbs, are all about pretending. Drama queens will be rewarded here; in these games you are *expected* to act up.

Even the most reserved member of the family, once pushed past his comfort barrier and onto the parlour floor, will often secretly thrill in putting on a silly voice or pretending to be a wheelbarrow. Indeed, many professional actors confess to being pathologically shy, finding a freedom in acting that they don't feel when being 'themselves'.

Whether you choose to ham it up or play it straight, we know you will enjoy your moment in the limelight.

TALENT QUEST

Like the Treasure Hunt, this is a game with limitless possibilities. A Talent Quest is especially fun with larger gatherings of family and friends. Plan it in advance and make up special categories and awards, or just organise it on the spot. Who needs *Pop Idol*, eh?

NUMBER OF PLAYERS	6 to 20
AGE	5 and up
YOU WILL NEED	Performers (props, music player, instruments, and paper and pens are all optional)
PLAYING TIME	30 to 120 minutes

OBJECT OF THE GAME
To sing, dance, recite, or act your heart out.

HOW TO PLAY
There are no rules whatsoever to holding a Talent Quest. Be as elaborate or simple as you wish; either way, you'll want one or two players to organise the event and MC it. Note: a carrot makes a good microphone.

Pick a few categories for players to enter: for example, funkiest hip-hop dance, most pompous Shakespeare recitation, slinkiest Elvis impression. Or select a single category, such as best on-the-spot poem about autumn leaves, or funniest stand-up comedy routine. Or just announce performers one at a time — 'Here's the Marvellously Melodious Mary!' — and let them strut whatever their stuff might be. Give contestants time to rehearse and warm up.

If you have time to plan ahead for a Talent Quest, consider printing up programs, setting up a stage with a curtain, and organising prizes or certificates. Perhaps a wooden spoon for the player whose talent has not yet shone through?

Last thing to consider is whether you are going to have judges. For a big group, it is great fun to a have a panel of two or three judges. Make them numbered squares from one to ten, so they can hold up their rating after each act. Or forget the judges and take an audience vote. Or don't rate the acts at all. Whichever way you go, the important thing is for players to have fun.

At the specified time, put on your lippie or leather pants, unplug the phone, and let the show begin ...

VARIATION
Divide players into two teams and play improvisational theatre, or Theatresports. Teams take turns performing dramatic scenes based on audience suggestions (for example, an airport farewell, or a tug-of-war) and are then rated by the audience or a panel of judges. The team with the most points after an agreed number of performances takes home the Tony.

WINK MURDER

You've got to love Wink Murder (also known as Killer and Lonely Ghost). It's an easy game that can be played anywhere, anytime, and the different roles in the game are all great fun. As Detective, you've got to be on full alert; as Murderer, you need to be devious and quick. But it's the victims who really get to act up — kids, particularly, love to draw out the death rattle.

NUMBER OF PLAYERS	6 to 12
AGES	6 and up
YOU WILL NEED	A small deck of cards comprising the same number of cards as players and including the Ace of Spades and the Ace of Hearts, players who can wink (check this out with younger children)
PLAYING TIME	10 minutes

OBJECT OF THE GAME

If Murderer, to murder as many players as you can before detection; if Detective, to find the murderer as quickly as possible.

HOW TO PLAY

Players need to be seated in a circle, either on the floor or around a table. One player shuffles the cards well and deals out one card per player, face down. Players peek at their cards. The person who has the Ace of Hearts declares himself and is Detective for that round. The rest of the players keep their cards secret, but the player who got the Ace of Spades is Murderer.

If you don't have a deck of cards to hand, use squares of paper in a hat. One should have 'M' for Murderer, and one 'D' for Detective, with the rest blank. Make sure they are all folded and look the same.

Players now sit and chat among themselves, looking around at one another as they do, until the Murderer manages to quickly catch the eye of a victim and wink at them. The victim slumps, feigning sudden death (as dramatically or silently as they wish), and is out of the game from then on, but can remain in the circle without speaking.

While the Detective's aim is to catch the Murderer with as few fatalities as possible, the Murderer's goal is to kill as many people as possible before detection. Therefore, she should try to do her winking when no one else is looking: she not only wants to evade the Detective but also doesn't want other players to avoid looking at her and being murdered. If another player does work out who the Murderer is before the Detective, he is not permitted to say anything. Obviously, no players other than the Murderer are permitted to wink at all during the game.

The killing spree continues until the Detective has correctly named the culprit. For six to eight players, he has two chances to get it right; for nine to 12 players, he has three chances.

Once the Murderer has been arrested and the other players brought back from the dead, it's time for the next round.

VARIATION

Vampire is an hilarious variation in which the murderer is replaced with a vampire who kills by subtly baring his teeth at a victim. In this version, you'll be struggling not to laugh as you take your last breaths. But before you embark, go around the circle and let everyone demonstrate their Vampire teeth, so you don't misconstrue Aunty Jenny's toothy smile.

ADVERBS

Also known as In the Manner of the Word, this is a fabulous game for budding young thespians, and can be hilarious when played by adults. Forget *The Bold and the Beautiful*; Adverbs is where you really get to ham it up.

NUMBER OF PLAYERS	4 to 12
AGE	6 and up
YOU WILL NEED	Actooooors!
PLAYING TIME	5 minutes per performance

OBJECT OF THE GAME

To guess which adverb the star player is acting out.

HOW TO PLAY

Someone volunteers to go first, and has to think of an adverb. The adverb can be as easy or difficult, as silly, strange, or obscure as you like. With children, for example, you might start out with adverbs like 'quickly', 'slowly', 'angrily', and 'slyly', but with older children and adults, you could have a try at 'manically', 'majestically', even 'childishly'.

Adverb selected, the metaphorical curtain now rises, and the player has to start acting out everyday tasks at the audience's request, but in the manner of the adverb: going to the toilet, winning a sprint race, reading a book. The performances continue until someone in the audience has correctly guessed the adverb, and it is then their turn to get up.

Picture someone ironing a shirt euphorically and you can imagine how fun this game can be.

VARIATIONS

When playing with very young children, call it 'Adjectives' — they are easier to grasp than Adverbs.

Adverbs can also be played in teams. Teams of two or more players get their heads together and take turns acting out given situations in the manner of the adverb. The winning team is the one to guess the other team's adverb fastest — though this might, in fact, reflect the losing team's superior acting skills.

SHADOW PLAY

Hang a white bed-sheet a couple of metres in front of a wall, and set up an extra-strong lamp behind it. The audience sits in a row in front of the sheet, with the lights off, while the performers step behind the sheet to act out small plays or tableaux. You can combine this with a very simple form of Charades and have the audience call out guesses as to what the shadow is doing ... Plaiting its hair? Baking a cake? Rope skipping?

I WENT TO TOWN

Also known as I Went to Paris, this is an old parlour game that, while simple in concept, is exceedingly difficult in execution. If you're no good at patting your head while rubbing your tummy, you're going to really struggle with this miming game. Much laughter guaranteed.

NUMBER OF PLAYERS	4 to 10
AGE	7 and up
YOU WILL NEED	Players
PLAYING TIME	10 minutes

OBJECT OF THE GAME
To perform a number of different actions simultaneously.

HOW TO PLAY
Players stand in a circle, and the youngest starts by commenting to the player to his left: 'I went to town.' The second player responds: 'What did you buy there?' The first player then answers with something that has a corresponding action. For example, 'a pair of shoes' might be accompanied by his feet moving up and down, as if walking. The remaining players have to copy this action and keep it up for the duration of the game.

I WENT TO TOWN TO BUY A HORSE

The second player now addresses the third player with 'I went to town ...', and the exchange is repeated, with the second player introducing a new movement. If she bought a new ring, it could entail a rippling of the fingers of the left hand, all the while continuing the walking movement. This is repeated right around the circle until all players are both moving their feet and rippling their fingers.

The game continues thus around the circle, with each player contributing another action. You can use your imagination here: think walking sticks, contact lenses, crunchy toffee, etc. When players are in full swing, their bodies occupied in six or more independent movements, it looks absolutely hilarious — and is surprisingly tiring.

As players slip up and make mistakes, they have to leave the circle. The last player to keep up this mental and physical feat wins the game.

THE NARRATOR

This is a superb improvisation game. It's fascinating to watch the way the storyteller and her characters interact and affect one another. And, of course, it's fun to see what kind of crazy stories different players come up with. This game is also known as The Typewriter.

NUMBER OF PLAYERS	4 to 10
AGE	7 and up
YOU WILL NEED	Players and a stopwatch (props are optional)
PLAYING TIME	10 minutes

OBJECT OF THE GAME
If you are Narrator, to tell a good story; if you are a character, to act it out.

HOW TO PLAY
Choose a player to be Narrator — roll a die if you having trouble deciding. You are in a powerful position as Narrator, but it is equally fun playing a character, and this way you get to influence the story from within.

The Narrator takes a seat, gets out an invisible typewriter, and pretends to start typing her story. From this point, she has exactly ten minutes to tell her story. First, she gives her actors a title for the story; for example, 'The Scary Clown'. Then, she tells each actor what part they will be playing, going into just enough detail to give the actor a starting point; for example, 'You are a little girl who is scared of clowns.' When everyone knows who they are, the Narrator tells them what happens first in the story; for example, 'A circus comes to town.' Then, it's improvisation time: the narrator sits back and lets the characters take over. This is not a miming game; monologues, tears, song, are all allowed.

During the ten minutes, however, the Narrator can interject at any time to introduce a scene change, alter the course of the story, add new details, kill off characters, or even introduce new ones (you might find yourself playing two or three parts). Characters must do whatever their Narrator tells them but can embellish and add freely. It is fascinating to watch how the actors and the Narrator interact to build the story.

When the ten minutes is nearing its end, the Narrator must try to bring the story to a neat close. Then, it's curtain call, and bouquets of roses all round.

WHO IS THE LEADER?

You need at least eight players for this game. Send one player out of the room, while the remaining players decide who will be Leader. The exiled player returns and stands in the middle of a circle formed by the other players. Whenever the Leader starts a new mime — for example, drinking a cup of tea — the other players have to copy; however, the aim is to conceal from the middle man where the action is starting. Obviously, the Leader will avoid starting a new mime when the middle man is looking directly at him, but it is also important that other players don't openly watch the Leader. When the middle man has correctly identified the Leader, he gets to swap places with him, and the game starts over.

MURDER IN THE DARK

Another murder-detective game made fun and exciting by being played in the scary dark. Overacting is essential.

NUMBER OF PLAYERS	6 to 12
AGE	8 and up
YOU WILL NEED	A small deck of cards (one per player, including the Ace of Hearts and Ace of Spades), and a very dark room
PLAYING TIME	15 minutes

OBJECT OF THE GAME

If Detective, to work out who has committed murder; if Murderer, to get away with it; if a civilian, to have fun and die dramatically.

HOW TO PLAY

Deal one card to each player. The player who gets the Ace of Hearts is the Detective, and the player who gets the Ace of Spades is the Murderer. Everyone else is a civilian — and in danger. (If you don't have cards, tear up small slips of paper, and mark 'M' on one, 'D' on another, and leave the rest blank. Pick them out of a hat.) Only the Detective reveals himself; the remaining players keep their identities secret.

To start the game, the Detective must leave the room, closing the door behind him.

Now for the fun: the lights are turned off, and the shuffling about begins. Note that it needs to be a very dark room: unless you have block-out curtains, the game is better played at night. The game works best when not only the Detective but also the civilians are unaware of who the Murderer is.

While people are stumbling about in the dark, the Murderer has to find a victim and tap her three times on the shoulder, after which the victim must let out a blood-curdling cry and fall to the ground. On hearing the scream, all other players must freeze in their positions, and only the Murderer can quickly move to another spot in the room.

When the Detective hears the scream, he counts slowly to ten, then rushes back in, turns the lights on, and finds the body. He then gets to interrogate all the other players. Some questions might include: What were you doing at the time the crime was committed? Did you notice anyone else acting suspiciously in the lead-up to the fatal moment? Who do you think is responsible for this atrocity? All players must answer the questions honestly, apart from the Murderer, who can lie freely (perhaps trying to incriminate someone else) except if challenged directly; that is, if asked, 'Are you the Murderer?' All players must answer this question truthfully; however, the Detective is only allowed to ask the question twice, so he needs to gather as much information as he can before accusing anyone directly.

If the Detective is unable to solve the crime, the player who got the Ace of Spades has gotten away with cold-blooded murder. Players then shuffle the cards and play again.

MAFIA

This is a terrific game in the tradition of Wink Murder, but is more complex and better suited to adults and older children. Also known as Assassin, this game was dreamt up in the psychology department of a Moscow University in 1986, and involves a struggle between an informed minority and an uninformed majority. Good group detective work is needed, as well as some real acting on the part of the baddies to conceal their identities. Have fun, and may goodness prevail.

NUMBER OF PLAYERS	6 to 16
AGE	8 and up
YOU WILL NEED	A small deck of cards comprising the same number of cards as players and including the Joker, and red and black cards in a ratio of roughly 2 to 1
PLAYING TIME	15 to 30 minutes

OBJECT OF THE GAME

If Mafia, to kill off as many Townspeople as you can; if Townspeople, to execute all the Mafia.

HOW TO PLAY

Cards are dealt to assign players' roles. The person who gets the Joker is the Mayor, and is the only person to declare themselves. The identities of the remaining players are kept secret. Players who get a black card are Mafiosi, while players with red cards are Townspeople. There should be roughly twice as many Townspeople as Mafiosi: for six to eight players, have two Mafiosi; for nine to 11 players, three Mafiosi; etc. If you don't have a pack of cards to hand, write the roles onto bits of paper and pick out of a hat.

Players sit in a circle (on the floor, at a table, on couches). The game commences with the Mayor, who acts as narrator for the game, telling everyone to close their eyes and go to sleep. So begins the first 'night' in the game. While the town is quietly sleeping, the mayor instructs the Mafiosi to open their eyes. The Mafiosi now all know who one another are, as does the Mayor, but the Townspeople don't know who are Mafiosi. Using eye contact, nodding, and shaking of heads, the Mafiosi decide on one Townsperson to murder, and they communicate this to the Mayor — silently, of course. The Mayor now instructs the Mafiosi to close their eyes and go back to sleep. Soon after, the Mayor instructs all players to open their eyes to a new dawn.

As players stretch and rub their eyes, the Mayor makes a grave announcement about the murder in the night, revealing which of the Townspeople has died. The dead Townsperson is now out of the game and cannot speak, but is permitted to stay in as a silent spectator for the remainder of the game. If you are Mayor, have fun with the announcement, making it as gruesome and detailed as you like ('Billy was found in the bath wearing only socks, with a fork sticking out of his head, and "Saturday Night Fever" on repeat on the stereo.').

Players now start asking each other questions and arguing about who they think might be acting suspiciously. The Mafia are doing their best here to conceal their true identities and act as shocked, outraged, and innocent as the rest. They will be trying to convince others that one of the Townspeople is guilty of the crime. This period of debate, of accusation and defence, is the most interesting part of the game.

By the end of the 'day' (say, five to ten minutes), the group as a whole — apart from the Mayor, who is all-seeing — has to vote on a player to be executed for the crime. The Mayor helps the group narrow the choice down to two suspects (or three, if you have heaps of players). Each player votes once and cannot vote for himself. Whoever gets the most votes is put to death, and is from thereon out of the game. Once the selected player has been despatched, they can reveal their role. Was a Townsperson innocently put to death, or was it a Mafioso? How many Mafiosi are left? (It's worth nothing that, in order to get a majority vote and save their own skins, there may be occasions when the Mafia have to betray one of their clan. Some people play with a silent vote so that this need never happen.)

Night falls again. While everyone is sleeping (eyes closed), the Mayor asks the remaining Mafia to open their eyes, and they repeat the process of the night before, deciding on one of the Townspeople to murder. They close their eyes again. Shortly thereafter, the sun rises, and the Mayor announces another murder, naming the victim. That person is now out of the game, but the remaining players have to talk and argue again, until another Mafia suspect has been voted out and executed. Did they get the right person, or was it a miscarriage of justice?

The game continues, with Townspeople murdered at night and suspected Mafia executed by day, until either all the Mafia are dead (goodness prevails) or the Mafia have outnumbered the Townspeople (run for cover).

VARIATION

Add into the mix a Detective who is allied with the Townspeople (make this the Ace of Hearts). During the nights, after the Mafia have done their kill and gone back to sleep and before the town wakes up, the Detective gets to 'wake up' alone and point at a suspect. The Mayor confirms if this suspect is Mafia. Where this additional element becomes very interesting is that the Detective can choose to reveal his role to the other Townspeople by day, which he might do to persuade the group of a particular suspect; but, if he does, he is likely to be killed by the Mafia the next night. He may choose, then, to use his extra knowledge to argue more forcefully against a particular suspect, but without showing he has insider knowledge. Furthermore, because the role of Detective is not automatically revealed at the beginning of the game, this opens up the possibility of false Detectives — players claiming to be Detective who are not, and who may be out to do more harm than good. The ultimate outcomes will depend on how well you are playing your parts.

CHARADES

Charades is a wonderful game to play with kids and equally fun at an adult dinner party. It is probably the most famous of the parlour games, and there are many variations, but all involve players performing pantomimes to represent words or phrases. The game detailed below is the 20th-century version, which includes movies and TV shows in its categories — poignant, considering TV has virtually killed the parlour game. Maybe, as a return tribute, we could all play a little Charades in the ad breaks.

NUMBER OF PLAYERS	4 to 12
AGE	9 and up
YOU WILL NEED	Players
PLAYING TIME	30 minutes

OBJECT OF THE GAME

To guess the name of the book, movie, song, TV show, play, character, phrase, or quote being acted out by the star player.

HOW TO PLAY

A player volunteers or is elected to begin. First, she has to think of the name of a book, film, song, TV show, play, character (famous person or fictional character), or a well-known phrase or quote.

She starts her turn by miming to the audience which of these seven categories she is acting out. (Throughout her turn she is not allowed to speak under any circumstances — short of a fire breaking out in the kitchen.)

There are some conventional mimes used to indicate the different categories:

- For a book, press the palms of your hands together, and then open them, hinged at the little fingers, as if opening a book.
- For a film, use your left hand to make a camera lens, and hold it up to your eye. Use your right hand to make circles in the air beside it, as if cranking an old-fashioned movie camera.
- For a song, hold up a microphone and mime singing.

- For a TV show, draw a big square TV screen. For a play, mime with both hands the pulling of the rope that opens the theatre curtains.
- For a character, put your hands on your hips, and then put up one finger for a male and two for a female. Finally, if you are going to mime a famous phrase or quote, make quote marks in the air with your fingers.

BOOK

FILM

SONG

T.V. SHOW

PLAY

CHARACTER

QUOTE

When a member of the audience has correctly identified the chosen category, the actor points to the person who gave the correct answer. This is how answers are affirmed throughout. The actor now holds up the appropriate number of fingers to indicate how many words there are in her subject, and the charades proper can begin.

Each word is acted out one at a time, in any order. The actor puts up the appropriate number of fingers to indicate which word she is going to act out first. If it is the third word, for example, she will put up three fingers.

For the miming, there are a couple of basic rules: in addition to remaining mute, the actor cannot draw letters in the air or point out words on paper. They can, however, indicate objects. If the phrase is a 'couch potato', for example, they can wave a potato about.

For short words, such as 'and', 'if', and 'to', the actor puts thumb and forefinger close together to mime that the word is short. These words are often guessed quickly, and the actor indicates as above when the right one is called out. Longer words can either be acted out in full or broken down into syllables. The number of syllables is indicated by laying the appropriate number of fingers on the opposite forearm: so, if it is three syllables, three fingers will be spread. If the actor puts two fingers on their forearm immediately after this, it means that they are going to act out the second syllable. If the word was 'pigsty', for example, the actor could indicate first that there were two syllables; then, they would indicate that they are acting out the first syllable; and finally, they would get on hands and knees to mime a pig. No animal noises allowed!

If it's a particularly hard word or syllable, the actor can mime another word that sounds like it. She does this by first tugging her earlobe — the mime for 'sounds like' — and then acting it out. When this word has been correctly identified, the audience has to guess what it sounded like.

Another useful convention is to put hands in the air, with palms facing one another, and move them in or out to indicate that the word needs either shortening or lengthening.

The game continues as the answer is put together, syllable by syllable, word by word. The winner is the person who guesses the entire answer first. It is then her turn to put on a charade.

VARIATION

Got a big group? Back in Victorian times, Charades was generally played in teams, with one-word answers and without specially coded mimes. For this traditional version, divide players into two or three teams, and have them go off to different corners or rooms in the house to get their act together. Each team has to come up with a word of two or more syllables that can be broken up and mimed: for example, in-habit-ant, deck-oar-ate, inn-true-shun, man-tell-piece, car-pet, drag-on-fly. Just coming up with the word can be challenging. After an agreed time — say, ten minutes — the teams return, and each takes turns miming their word, syllable by syllable, until one of the other teams has guessed correctly. Dress-ups and props are optional.

Man is a make-believe animal.
He is never so truly himself as when he is acting a part.
— William Hazlitt

GAMES WITH A STRAIGHT FACE

If you are tense and tired and taking things way too seriously (typical signs of life in the modern world, for adults and children alike), what you probably need is to excavate your sense of humour from the debris of the day, and have yourself a big, hearty, knee-slapping, whoop of a laugh. The physical and emotional health benefits are immense, and have been well documented (see p. 128).

A whole bunch of Victorian parlour games were based upon participants keeping a straight face while doing daft things: the first to smile would be the loser. These games are deceptively simple and surprisingly fun, and will be enjoyed by players of all ages. They don't require deep thinking or great general knowledge, but they make us laugh — a lot.

THE INTERROGATOR

Also known in the days of the parlour as Pig's Feet and The Birthday Present, this is a great game for very young children and their silly parents. Ah, the simple joys.

NUMBER OF PLAYERS	4 to 10
AGE	4 and up
YOU WILL NEED	A good imagination and a poker face
PLAYING TIME	5 minutes

OBJECT OF THE GAME

To keep a straight face throughout.

HOW TO PLAY

Players sit in a circle, and a player is elected to go first as the Interrogator. The group then decides on a silly word or phrase that will be the answer to every question the Interrogator asks. 'Pig's feet', 'dog's bottom', 'warm fish milkshake', or 'pickled egg' are just a few of the infinite possibilities.

The Interrogator then has to go round the circle, asking each player a different question, to which they must answer with the chosen phrase. It can be any question; for example, 'What do you love most in the world?' which would be answered seriously with, 'Warm fish milkshake.'

The players answering the questions are not allowed to laugh, or even smile, during this process. When the first one inevitably cracks, he has to swap places with the Interrogator and seek his mirthful revenge.

WARM FISH MILKSHAKE

THROWING THE SMILE

This is a fabulous parlour game. There is something graceful, almost poetic, in Throwing the Smile: a twinkle of Marcel Marceau in your very own living room. Take out your camera to capture this one on film.

NUMBER OF PLAYERS	4 to 10
AGE	5 and up
YOU WILL NEED	Plenty of self-control
PLAYING TIME	5 minutes

OBJECT OF THE GAME
To smile only when it is your turn to do so.

HOW TO PLAY
Seated in a circle, the youngest player begins by smiling at each of the other straight-faced players. After a bit, she literally wipes the smile from her face, with the back of her hand, and pretends to throw it to any other player of her choice. The recipient of the smile has to reach up, catch it, and put it on; then, after wearing the smile for a few moments, they wipe it off and toss it to someone else.

Anyone who smiles out of turn must leave the game immediately. Once out, however, the expelled players can try to move the game along by entertaining, with silly faces, those players left in the circle.

The last poker-faced player to remain in the game wins.

THE GREAT MOGUL

Younger siblings particularly relish taking their turn as the Great Mogul. You can throw some dress-ups into the mix here, too. Our kids like to fashion themselves a turban, or sometimes a metal bowl regally placed on the top of the head.

NUMBER OF PLAYERS	4 to 10
AGE	5 and up
YOU WILL NEED	Players, dress-ups optional
PLAYING TIME	5 minutes

OBJECT OF THE GAME

To keep a straight face when sitting at the feet of the Great Mogul.

HOW TO PLAY

Players elect the Great Mogul, and he perches regally on a stool or chair that is his throne. If he wants to, he can don some mogulish attire. All the other players seat themselves at his feet and proceed to address the Mogul in fawning tones, perhaps while massaging his tootsies: 'Great Mogul, I adore and worship thee, and will serve thee in any way thy may see fit ...'

All of this must be done in a very solemn fashion and, throughout, the Great Mogul must make the most grotesque faces he possibly can to make his subjects laugh. If they laugh, they are expelled from his service. The last servant left sitting at his feet is the winner and gets to take the place of the Great Mogul for the next round.

IS LAUGHTER THE BEST MEDICINE?

'Frame your mind to mirth and merriment,
which bars a thousand harms and lengthens life,'
— Shakespeare, *The Taming of the Shrew*

It is a long and widely held view, found in early scripture, literature, and science, that merriment is medicine to the body and soul, and laughter is now treated quite seriously as a complementary medicine. But what are the health benefits of laughter, and how do we get them?

WHAT HAPPENS TO YOU WHEN YOU LAUGH?

Many claims have been made about the therapeutic benefits of laughter. In a major review of the scientific literature on the health benefits of laughter, Mary Bennett and Cecile Lengacher concluded that a hearty laugh does increase heart rate, respiratory rate and depth, and oxygen consumption. In other words, it makes you breathe deeper and increases oxygen supply to your blood.

The review also confirmed that after chortling, you can expect a decrease in heart and respiratory rate, an increase in muscle relaxation, and a decrease in blood pressure. In layman's language, once you've stopped cacking yourself, you will be more relaxed than you were before you heard the joke. In increasing physical relaxation, laughter can also alleviate physical pain.

There are claims that laughter improves immune function, though Bennett and Lengacher suggested that further research is needed to work out exactly what mechanism could be at work here, and what effect laughter might have on specific disease processes. But the review of available research concluded that laughter definitely improves our mental health, helps us cope better with stress, makes us less lonely, and improves self-esteem.

Ha! So there!

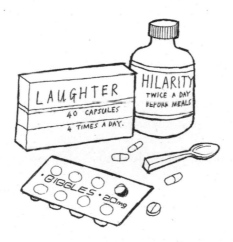

WHAT'S SO FUNNY?

Having ascertained that it's good to laugh, there seems to be a miserable agreement that people across the world laugh significantly less now than they did 50 years ago. In response to this mirthless state of affairs, an entire laughing industry has sprung up in recent years, like some great jack-in-the-box. We now have hospital clowns, qualified laughter practitioners, courses in laughter yoga (we're serious), and neighbourhood laughter clubs that encourage you to stand in a circle and fake it till you make it.

But well before the invention of laughter yoga, families were doing it for themselves, at home and for free. They were playing games; and playing games makes you laugh.

So, by all means, read the funny book, and wander up to your local park for the Saturday-morning laughter club; but, for a healthful giggle that will improve your emotional and physical wellbeing and family unity, you need not go further than a spot of Flip the Kipper or a round of Throw Your Smile.

Laugh, or your money back!

THE SCULPTOR

Another silly one — enjoy!

NUMBER OF PLAYERS	4 to 10
AGE	5 and up
YOU WILL NEED	Willing participants
PLAYING TIME	5 minutes

OBJECT OF THE GAME

To keep a straight face while standing in a ridiculous contorted position.

HOW TO PLAY

Players stand scattered about a room in no particular pattern. One player is nominated as the Sculptor, and he wanders around the room arranging each player, one at a time, into silly positions — the more ridiculous, the better. Perhaps have Mum bending over sniffing Dad's bottom? Players must then hold the postures until the Sculptor has shaped the lot. Throughout, the players being sculpted are not allowed to smile, even slightly, or to close their eyes to avoid the scene before them.

As well as making everyone look ridiculous, the Sculptor can do anything extra he likes to make people laugh, short of touching them. As soon as a player smiles, she is out of the game and has to sit down. The Sculptor can do a second circuit if need be, repositioning his subjects. The last player left in is the Sculptor next time round.

HAGOO

This game originated with the Tlingit Indians of Alaska; 'hagoo' means 'come here'. This is a team game, so one for bigger groups. Which side has the most self-control?

NUMBER OF PLAYERS	8 to 20
AGE	6 and up
YOU WILL NEED	Plenty of self-control
PLAYING TIME	10 to 15 minutes

OBJECT OF THE GAME

To keep a straight face throughout, and to make members of the opposing team smile.

HOW TO PLAY

Players are divided into two teams of equal size, which line up with each player facing another, about four feet apart, to form a corridor. One player from each team, at opposite ends of the lines, steps forward, then turns to face their opponent down the length of the gauntlet. To begin, they need to bow and loudly challenge one another, 'Hagoo!' They then have to walk slowly towards one another without breaking eye contact and without smiling. When they reach the middle, they turn and walk backwards, still eyeballing each other, until they get to the end of the line.

During this time, other members of the teams can try to make the challenger from the opposing team smile, but they have to do so silently and without touching them. And, obviously, they don't want to inadvertently make their own challenger laugh.

If players make it all the way to the end of the line without smiling, they get to rejoin their own team. You will be amazed at how difficult this is. If a challenger smiles, however, they have to join the opposing team. If both challengers smile, they simply swap places.

The next two challengers step out for their turn, and the game continues until all players have had their go, at which point the team with the most players wins. Or you can play until there is only one team left.

GAMES FOR RAINY DAYS

'Millions long for immortality who don't know what to do with themselves on a rainy Sunday afternoon,' observed British writer Susan Ertz. If you suffer from this predicament, read on for some answers, and may you live a long and playful life. The lives of modern families tend to be so frantic, however, that a rainy day comes as a small gift, an opportunity to do less: to play and potter and reconnect.

All parlour games are good for rainy days, but the unifying theme in this section is motion: these are indoor games that allow you to expend some energy and get the endorphins going within the comfort of your own parlour. Some are more vigorous than others, some are competitive, and others plain silly. These games are perfect for long days confined indoors (by the heat, humidity, or wind, if not the rain), or for mid-afternoons on a Sunday, when it's time to haul the children off the computer and get their bodies and minds functioning again.

Feeling sluggish? Seedy? Step up for some Group Juggling.

FLIP THE KIPPER

We love this game. It is absurdly simple, and yet children and adults seem to take equal pleasure in it and become hilariously competitive. We learnt it from an octogenarian named Rose at the Norfolk Bowling Club in England, who was taught it by her grandmother.

NUMBER OF PLAYERS	3 to 10
AGE	3 and up
YOU WILL NEED	Newspaper and scissors, pen, books for flapping
PLAYING TIME	10 minutes

OBJECT OF THE GAME
To get your kipper over the finish line first.

HOW TO PLAY
To make the kippers, draw a simple fish shape onto an old newspaper and then cut around it (through the layers). The fish should be roughly 40cm long. You should now have a nice stack of newspaper kippers; give one to each player and have them write their names on the fish, for later identification.

You will need to have a decent-sized floor space cleared of any obstructions. Create a start and finish line at either end of the room. Make it as long as you can.

Players each need a book to flap: this creates the wind to propel their kipper along. Try to use books of roughly the same size to make it fair. (We use matching books from a set of school readers; magazines would also be good.)

Players line up in a row with their kippers. At 'go', they flap their books wildly to race their kippers across the floor and over the finish line. The first kipper over the line wins.

NO-HANDS CEREAL

Pour a bowl of cereal for each contestant; any type of cereal will do, but it must be the same type for all players. Line the bowls up in a row on a bench or table. Players proceed to eat the cereal without using their hands. The player who makes the least mess — check shirtfronts and tabletops for crumbs — is the winner. To make it harder and messier, add milk.

BLOW FOOTBALL

Another windy game. Also known as Blow Ball and, poetically, The Tuft on the Table, the player or team with the most puff wins. Though there isn't any running around here, the blowing sure wears you out.

NUMBER OF PLAYERS	2 to 6
AGE	4 and up
YOU WILL NEED	Players, a table, a tuft of cotton wool or a ping-pong ball, and four boxes of matches (or four other small objects)
PLAYING TIME	5 minutes

OBJECT OF THE GAME
To score goals by blowing the ball through your opponent's goalposts.

HOW TO PLAY
If there are two players, one player stands on either side of the table; if there are teams, an equal number of players stand on each side. Either a ping-pong ball or a tuft of cotton wool (as they used in the 19th-century parlour) is placed in the centre of the table, and the boxes of matches (or nail polish, or whatever) are placed at either team's side to make goalposts.

At the word 'go', players blow as hard as they can to propel the ball across the table and through their opponents' goalposts. No touching!

The first side to reach ten goals wins the match.

DUCK, DUCK, GOOSE

Known in Minnesota as Duck, Duck, Grey Duck, this is a lovely tag game, great for parties. Simple but suspenseful, the only skill required is speed and quick reactions. Clear the floor for this one.

NUMBER OF PLAYERS	6 to 12
AGE	4 and up
YOU WILL NEED	Players and a decent-sized room
PLAYING TIME	15 minutes

OBJECT OF THE GAME

To be the first to the empty seat.

HOW TO PLAY

One player volunteers, or is elected, to be the fox, and the rest of the players kneel in a circle on the floor, facing inward. The fox then walks slowly around the circle, tapping each successive player on the head, and naming them 'Duck', 'Duck', 'Duck', until, at any chosen moment, the fox taps a player and shouts 'Goose!' The goose then jumps up and chases the fox around the circle, trying to catch him, while the fox tries to escape and get all the way round and into the empty space in the circle left by the goose.

If the fox manages to get back to the gap in the circle and sit down without being caught, the goose takes the fox's place and the game begins again. However, if the goose catches the fox before he's filled the gap, the fox has to start his circling again. The farmyard frolics go on for as long as people are having fun.

VARIATION

In this version, known as I Wrote a Letter to My Love (also known as Drop the Handkerchief), a player walks slowly around the outside of the circle, touching each player with his hanky while chanting the following verse, roughly to the tune of 'Yankee Doodle Dandy': 'I wrote a letter to my love, but on the way I dropped it. Someone must have picked it up, and put it in their pocket.' This player then drops the hanky behind one of the other player's backs and sets off running. The player behind whose back the hanky was deposited has to jump up and chase the first player around the circle. The last one back to the vacant space has to be lovelorn poet next time round.

THE SEA IS AGITATED

Also known as Sea and Fishes, this game is a close cousin of Musical Chairs. As in circle games like Duck, Duck, Goose, players race to get to a chair knowing there will always be one player left out. It's also a good memory exercise, for the Sea has to remember the names of all the fish.

NUMBER OF PLAYERS	6 to 12
AGE	4 and up
YOU WILL NEED	Players, a decent-sized room, and chairs for all players save one
PLAYING TIME	15 minutes

OBJECT OF THE GAME

To not be left without a chair.

HOW TO PLAY

Chairs are placed in a circle, facing inward. One player volunteers, or is elected, to be the 'Sea', while the rest are seated. The Sea gives each person in the circle the name of a fish — mackerel, snapper, shark, sardine, cod, flathead, tuna, salmon, etc. She then wanders round the outside of the seats, murmuring, 'The sea is agitated, the sea is agitated,' over and over. At some point, she must suddenly call out the name of one of the fish, for example, 'tuna'. At the call of his name, 'tuna' must rise and follow behind the Sea, also murmuring, 'The sea is agitated, the sea is agitated,' over and over.

The Sea then calls on a second fish to join in the serenade, and then a third, and so on, until all the fish are in motion, swimming around the seats, chanting. This goes on until, at any chosen and unexpected moment, the Sea suddenly calls out, 'The sea is calm!' upon which all the players, including the Sea, rush to sit on one of the seats.

Of course, there are not enough, and whoever is left out becomes the Sea for the next round.

VARIATIONS

Another lovely variation of this game is called The General Post. Chairs are set in a circle, facing inward, and all seated players choose a country for a name. The player without a seat stands in the middle of the circle and is Postman. When he announces that he has brought a letter from one country to another, the players representing those two countries have to jump up and exchange places. As they are doing this, the Postman must try to slip onto one of the seats. If he fails, he has to keep naming two countries until he succeeds, at which time the player left without a seat becomes Postman (and the old Postman takes over his country).

For Musical Chairs, put chairs in a row, alternating which way they face (front or back) with one chair fewer than the number of players. Someone outside the game needs to operate the music player (or play an instrument) with their back turned to the group. While the music is playing, the players dance around in a circle outside the chairs (not too close). When the music stops, at an unexpected moment, they all rush to get onto a chair. Whoever is left out has to leave the game, and one chair is removed for the next round. Repeat until there are only two players and one chair left. The first person to the final chair is winner.

In Musical Statues, take away the chairs, and the last person to freeze like a statue when the music stops goes out. Continue until there is only one player remaining.

In Musical Bumps, the last person to sit down on the floor when the music stops goes out. And so on.

DEAD FISH

Also known as Sleeping Lion and Resting Tigers, this is a sweet, meditative game to play when the family needs winding down. Kids love playing it because the only skill required is the ability to stay still. Warning: adults will fall asleep playing this game.

NUMBER OF PLAYERS	3 to 10
AGE	4 and up
YOU WILL NEED	A floor with carpet or a rug
PLAYING TIME	10 minutes

OBJECT OF THE GAME
To stay perfectly still the longest.

HOW TO PLAY
All but one of the players lie down on the floor with their eyes closed, keeping as still as possible, as if they were dead fish. The remaining player is the fisherman. The fisherman moves quietly around the room looking for signs of life in the fish. If he spies any movement, he walks over to that

fish and taps it on the back. This fish is then 'caught', and has to go to a designated spot (the corner or the couch, say, to wait until the game is over). Daring fish might sneak their eyes open and wriggle about when the fisherman's back is turned. But watch out: if he turns around quickly, you're dinner!

The last dead fish is the winner and gets to be fisherman next time round. If you have a bunch of very lifeless fish and the game is lagging, you can allow the fisherman to try to awaken his fish by talking to them or through a little gentle poking.

BALLOON VOLLEYBALL

Another very simple indoor game that will have you running around panting. This was played, once upon a time, with an inflated pig's bladder.

NUMBER OF PLAYERS	2 to 8
AGE	5 and up
YOU WILL NEED	One balloon, and a piece of rope or string
PLAYING TIME	10 minutes

OBJECT OF THE GAME
To keep the balloon in the air.

HOW TO PLAY
Use the rope or string to set up a 'net', by tying it across the middle of your playing space using chairs, table legs, whatever. Rifle through your party supply to find a balloon, and blow it up. Position between one and four players on either side of the net.

A referee throws the ball up in the middle of the net, and then players on either side try to hit it over the net towards their opponents. If the ball hits the ground on either side, that's one point for the opposing team. Points are also scored if your opponents take more than two hits to get the balloon back over the net.

The first player or team to reach ten points wins the game.

VARIATION

For Balloon Tennis, play as above but with just four players, and use wooden spoons to hit the balloon over the net.

KNOCK 'EM OFF!

To spice up a pillow fight, that favourite sibling pastime, have opponents stand opposite one another on upturned buckets, crates, or stacks of telephone books. Obviously, you'll want to take basic safety precautions, so play away from sharp corners and, if possible, on a rug or carpet. Use pillows to try to knock each off your perches. Last one up wins.

Otherwise, try your standard pillow fight in a pitch-black room — it becomes something really special.

MUFFIN-PAN TOSS

Forget Tiddlywinks: here is a rough-and-ready game using a muffin pan and some coins. Easy to set up and plastic-free, it is also great for hand–eye coordination and mental arithmetic, and is heaps of fun.

NUMBER OF PLAYERS	2 to 6
AGE	6 and up
YOU WILL NEED	A muffin pan (if you don't have one, use an egg carton); five coins for each player (or nuts, legumes, buttons, etc.), paper, marker pens, scissors, and a matchbox
PLAYING TIME	15 minutes

OBJECT OF THE GAME

To score the most points over three rounds by getting your counters into the muffin holes.

HOW TO PLAY

Take a piece of A4 paper and fold it lengthways in three; then, fold it in four the opposite way, so that you have a small square comprising 12 layers of paper. Draw a circle with your texta, then cut around it. Ta-daah! Twelve paper discs.

In large writing, label each disc so that they number zero through to twelve. Put these discs randomly into the bottoms of the muffin holes, then position the pan at the far end of the rug or table on which you will be playing, and use a matchbox beneath the far edge to give it a slight tilt. Players have five coins, or other counters, each.

Create an offing at least 1.5m back from the pan, and let the youngest begin. One at a time, he must throw his coins towards the muffin pan, hoping to get them into the high-scoring holes. After he has thrown his five coins, he must add up his score for that round, take his coins back, and then it is the next player's turn.

Play continues for three rounds, so each player has 15 tosses all up, and the cumulative scores are compared to find the winner.

Take out the paper discs, and pop them somewhere safe for next time.

SCISSORS, PAPER, STONE

This is a quick game for two people, or it can be used to resolve arguments instead of tossing a coin. At the word 'go', players put forward their dominant hand in one of three positions: to represent scissors (using index and middle fingers), paper (hand flat), or stone (in a fist).

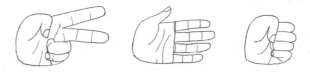

In each pair there will be a winner, according to the following rules. Note that, depending on the combination, all three positions can both win and lose:

- Scissors cuts paper, so scissors wins.
- Paper covers stone, so paper wins.
- Stone blunts scissors, so stone wins.
- If you both flash the same shape, go again.

REBOUND

This is a low-key ball game that is less about aim than about getting exactly the right strength to your delivery. It takes about two seconds to set up, but will occupy you for a lot longer.

NUMBER OF PLAYERS	2 to 10
AGE	6 and up
YOU WILL NEED	A ball, a coloured thread or ribbon, and a ruler
PLAYING TIME	10 minutes

OBJECT OF THE GAME
To roll the ball closest to the coloured line.

HOW TO PLAY

Lay the coloured thread or ribbon on the floor about 50cm in front of, and parallel to, a wall. This is where you want your ball to come to rest.

Players get back behind the line at an agreed distance, say 1.5m, and take turns rolling the ball against the wall, so that it rebounds towards the line. Use the ruler to measure how far the ball is from the ribbon. The player whose ball gets closest to the line wins the round.

Play a match and see who wins the most over several rounds. It is interesting how quickly your aim can improve; the person who starts out best may soon lose their Rebound lead.

PASS THE ORANGE

Another absurd game is Pass the Orange. You will find yourself trying very hard to win at something completely ridiculous. This is a team game for larger groups.

NUMBER OF PLAYERS	8 to 20
AGE	6 and up
YOU WILL NEED	Players and two oranges
PLAYING TIME	10 minutes

OBJECT OF THE GAME

To help your team pass the orange up and down the line the fastest.

HOW TO PLAY

Players get into two equal teams; if there is someone left over, they can be umpire and watch out for any cheating. The teams get into two straight lines, facing one another, and the opponents at the top end each put an orange between their feet.

At the word 'go', team members have to pass the orange down the line but only using their feet. This is as tricky as it sounds. If the orange is dropped and rolls away, the player who dropped it has to pick it up again, using their feet only, and rejoin the line where they were. If need be, they can get down on their bottoms.

The first team to get the orange all the way to the end of the line and then back again to the first player wins.

VARIATIONS

This game is also played with team members passing the orange using only their neck and chin, hands clasped behind backs. We played this version for the first time at a 21st-birthday party. What a delicious getting-to-know-you game.

An extra challenge is to make this a straight-faced game. Try playing Pass the Orange with serious expressions. If someone smiles, they have to wait out for a count of ten seconds before resuming play, allowing the other team to get ahead.

We adults need to remind ourselves again and again that the more responsible and grown-up and serious we all become, the more vital it is that we can, at will, rediscover our giggliest naughtiest selves.
— Julie Myerson, in *The Observer*, 2008

THE MATCHBOX GAME

This game is plain silly, but also fun, and requires good physical coordination and a little ingenuity. If you have especially long arms, you won't do well at it.

NUMBER OF PLAYERS	2 to 6
AGE	7 and up
YOU WILL NEED	An outer part of a matchbox for each player
PLAYING TIME	5 minutes

OBJECT OF THE GAME

To be the first to get the matchbox wedged on your nose.

HOW TO PLAY

Players get down on the floor on elbows and knees, with elbows actually touching knees, and place their matchboxes at a distance in front of them that is just beyond the reach of their outstretched fingers when forearms are flat to the floor. All in position? Good. You are about to engage in an act of simultaneous stupidity.

At 'go', players have to put their hands behind their backs and then try to get the matchbox onto their nose without moving forward on their knees. This is as hard as it sounds, but it is possible, we assure you.

The first person to sit up with the matchbox firmly on their snout is the winner.

STORK CONTEST

Put a tin can (full of beans, tomatoes, whatever) on the floor for each player to perch on. Hop on, standing on one foot with the other tucked up behind. Wear shoes or you'll hurt your feet. The stork who can stand the longest wins. Some adults can't manage this at all.

SLY SIMON SAYS

Also known as Thumbs Up, this is a great game to play when you're sitting around twiddling your thumbs. It's more a mental contest than a physical one: doing the opposite of what you're told to do is hard and, after a few rounds, this game tends to be frustrating for younger children. Pit adults against older children, however, and see who can keep it up the longest.

NUMBER OF PLAYERS	4 to 10
AGE	7 and up
YOU WILL NEED	Players who have both their thumbs
PLAYING TIME	10 minutes

OBJECT OF THE GAME
To stay in the game the longest by doing the opposite of what Sly Simon says.

HOW TO PLAY
Players sit round a table with their hands resting on the tabletop in front of them. One player gets to be Sly Simon and calls out instructions to players on how to position their hands. There are four possible positions: thumbs up, thumbs down, thumbs in, and thumbs out.

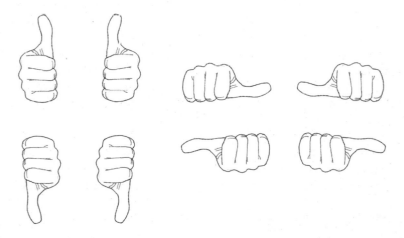

The catch is that, when Sly Simon calls one of these out, players have to immediately do the opposite. For example, if he calls out 'thumbs in', players have to turn their hands so that their thumbs are pointing out. If told to put thumbs down, players have to put thumbs up, etc.

Sly Simon can start off slowly but then fire instructions with increasing rapidity. (Tip: it can throw players off if he sometimes repeats the same instruction twice, or even three times, in a row.)

When a player puts his hands into the wrong position, he is out of the game. The last player in is the winner.

THUMB WRESTLING

Two players lock their right hands together (or left, if they are both left-handed) using their fingers, but keeping their thumbs free and pointing upwards. At 'go', the wrestling begins. The aim is to squish your enemy's thumb down flat with yours and hold it there for the count of three seconds. If they wriggle their thumb out before the count is up, the game continues. There can be no arm-twisting or sneaky use of other fingers (or else the offending player faces immediate disqualification). Make it a match and see who wins the most wrestles over five games.

GROUP JUGGLING

This is a favourite corporate team-building exercise, but don't let that put you off. Group Juggling is awesome fun, and the more you do it, the better you get. When you get really good, you can bring out the knives ... well, maybe not.

NUMBER OF PLAYERS	4 to 8
AGE	7 and up
YOU WILL NEED	One ball per player (or a pair of balled-up socks, a potato, an orange, etc.)
PLAYING TIME	15 minutes

OBJECT OF THE GAME

To work together to keep all the balls in the air.

HOW TO PLAY

Players start in a circle, and the first ball is introduced. Now, you have to establish a throwing pattern. You can't throw it to the person next to you (that would be boring), but have players hold up their hands until all players have received the ball once, and then start over. Repeat the same pattern until everyone knows who is throwing it to them and who they need to throw it to. Then, introduce the next ball.

Each time you master the juggle with the extra ball, bring in another one. Rhythm (and ball skills) is vital here. Aim to practise your group juggle until you can juggle with the same number of balls as players. And, if you're looking for the next challenge, start introducing balls with different throwing patterns.

KOTTABOS

Kottabos was a game of skill played in ancient Greece in the fourth and fifth centuries BC. The object was to toss at a target the sediment, or lees, from the bottom of your wine glass. Often, players would utter the name of their beloved as they tossed the lees, attempting to divine fate: if the wine met its target, love was just around the corner. It was acknowledged by the commentators of the time that there was a risk involved in playing too many games of Kottabos: excessive drunkenness.

FANCY PICKING PLUMS, OR SHALL WE STRIP JACK NAKED?

GAMES OF CARDS, DICE, MARBLES, AND KNUCKLEBONES

It doesn't take much to have a good time. We know it, but sometimes we forget; and who could blame us when there is so much on offer wherever we look? All the promises out there of fun to be had, pleasure and satisfaction, if we just buy this and that. Drive this car, wear these sunglasses, drink this soda — it'll be a blast! Picture it: the wind in your hair, the admiring looks, a sparkle in your teeth …

The elderly butcher from our local shopping strip, enlisted by us to collect knucklebones from his legs of lamb, recalled his childhood in northern Italy. 'We didn't have lot of money,' he explained, rubbing two fingers together fruitlessly. 'We used to play with anything. A stick, a rock, bones, just what we got. No problem.'

No problem, indeed. Here are a bunch of diverse, and diverting, games you can play with a pack of cards, some dice, marbles, and a few old bones. You probably have some of these things in the back of your dresser right now. Get them out. Dust them off. Enjoy.

GAMES OF CARDS

Playing cards are believed to have originated in China in the tenth century, entering Europe in the 14th century via the Islamic empire, where the four-suited deck evolved. Back then, cards were individually hand painted and found only in the parlours of the very wealthy. A medieval cards night would have been a major social event: bring on the pheasant and spiced wine! By the early 15th century, however, Germans had started printing them with wood cuts, and cards quickly went into mass production, crossing the class barrier and slowly fanning out across the new world.

Different European countries adopted different suits. German playing cards were adorned with hearts, leaves, bells, and acorns, while in Spain, they played with coins, cups, swords, and clubs. But it was from French designs that our modern-day English playing cards were derived. At one time, the King of Hearts was said to represent Charlemagne; the King of Diamonds, Julius Caesar; the King of Clubs, Alexander the Great; and the King of Spades, King David from the Bible. Cards travelled with the British to their colonies, and Americans began making their own around 1800. It was then that cards with rounded corners, varnished surfaces, and double-headed illustrations appeared (to save the nuisance of always righting them). Americans also gave us the Joker.

But, to put the potted history to one side, playing cards have been enduringly popular the world over because they give rise to an unending number and range of games. What we offer you here is the merest sampling, but it includes some fantastic family favourites, including games for young children new to cards, as well as for older children ready for more complex strategic thinking. Bear in mind that card games always look more complicated on paper than they are, so our advice is to get playing and work out what you're doing as you go along. We never score the first few hands of a new game.

Due to limitations of space, we are assuming a basic familiarity with a deck of playing cards (we are hoping you at least know what they look like when you rifle through your dresser drawer), though some commonly used terms are explained below. Unless otherwise specified, remove Jokers from the pack and treat the Ace as the lowest card. The games get progressively harder, with the balance gradually tipping from luck to skill — though most involve a combination. We take our inspiration from Robert Louis Stevenson: 'Life is not a matter of holding good cards but of playing a poor hand well.'

If you love these card games and want more, we highly recommend the classic *Official Rules of Card Games*, edited by Albert H. Morehead. First published in 1887, this card-players' bible has had more editions than we've had years on this earth. Look for it in your local op shop.

IS THAT A TRICK IN YOUR HAND? AND OTHER COMMON CARD TERMS

DECK/PACK: the full 52 playing cards

STOCK/STOCKPILE: the un-dealt portion of the pack that may be used during the course of play

DISCARD PILE: cards discarded onto a pile and sometimes accessed again during play

HAND: the set of cards you are dealt to play with

SUIT: one of the sets into which the cards are divided (Hearts ♥, Diamonds ♦, Clubs ♣, and Spades ♠)

RANK: the ordinal number position of a card in its suit; for example, for the Seven of Diamonds, 'seven' is the rank and 'diamonds' the suit. The usual order of cards is: Ace, two, three, four, five, six, seven, eight, nine, ten, Jack, Queen, King

ACE LOW/HIGH: in most games, ace is the lowest card in the suit, but in some it is the highest; assume lowest, unless otherwise specified

PICTURE CARD: a king, queen, or jack

NUMBER CARD: two through to ten

TRICK: a round of cards where one is contributed by each player; also refers to the package of these cards when gathered together, for example, 'Peter won four tricks.'

TRUMP: for any card of a suit that has been ordained 'trumps', in any given trick, cards of this suit will beat all other non-trump cards in the pack, no matter the rank

WHAT'S THE DEAL? 'CUTTING THE PACK', AND A LITTLE LESSON IN ETIQUETTE

There are two methods of, and functions to, 'cutting the pack'. Firstly, we cut the pack to decide who will be dealer. The pack is spread out face down, and each player selects a card and turns it over. The player with the highest card deals first.

After the dealer has shuffled the cards (see p. 165 for six ways to shuffle cards), the player to his right cuts the pack again — this time, to ensure there is no untoward cheaty behaviour going on. The player separates the pack into two parts, at a random point, and then puts the top part below the bottom, thereby reversing their order. The dealer can now continue with the job of dealing, starting with the person to his left.

Of course, in a family situation, you can choose to forgo these conventions. The youngest or keenest in your family might always get the job of doling out cards. On the other hand, it can be educational to do things the proper way.

If you were to listen to the wonderful Albert Morehead, here is what else you would advise your children on the etiquette of dealing:

1. Sit erect at the table, maintain a quiet bearing, avoid nervous habits. When someone else is dealing it is best to sit back and wait until the deal is fully completed before picking up one's hand.

2. Practice handling the deck of cards. An appearance of clumsiness in shuffling and dealing gives a bad impression of one's ability to play the game: People associate awkwardness of one sort with awkwardness or ineptness of other sorts.

Yep. Good luck with that.

SNAP

You can't talk about parlours and families and cards without mentioning Snap. For many of us, it was our very first card game, and it is still a great one to start kids off with. We include it here for those, like us, whose memories may need refreshing. While very simple, Snap does require concentration, dexterity, and quick reactions — good skills for any situation. Because it is fast and furious, there are times when adults may need to act as referees, especially in games between siblings.

NUMBER OF PLAYERS	2 to 6
AGE	4 and up
YOU WILL NEED	One pack of cards for 2 to 3 players; two packs for 4 to 6 players
PLAYING TIME	10 to 20 minutes

OBJECT OF THE GAME
To win all the cards.

HOW TO PLAY
The entire pack is dealt out evenly among players, with cards placed face down in a pile in front of each player. No one looks at their cards. The player to the left of the dealer starts by turning over the top card from her pile and placing it face up beside her stock to form a discard pile. It is important that players turn cards over quickly, and without peeking, so that everyone gets to see them at the same time.

Play moves clockwise around the circle, until someone turns over a card that matches in rank the top card on another player's discard pile (for example, a Seven of Spades matches a Seven of Hearts). When this happens, the first person to cry 'Snap!' wins the contents of both discard piles, which she places face down at the bottom of her stock. She then turns over the top card of her stock and play continues.

If a player's face-down cards run out during the game but she still has a discard pile, she can stay in and try to 'snap' up more cards; but, if she misses the next match, she is out of the game. If no match is made before the other players also run out of face-down cards, all players shuffle their packs and start again. Note: a player who calls 'Snap!' at the wrong time has to give one card to each of the other players as a penalty.

The first player to snap up all the cards in the pack wins.

VARIATION

To play Slapjack, deal out as for Snap but, instead of individual discard piles, players take turns to place their cards onto one central pile. When a Jack of any suit appears, all players have to slap a hand down as fast as they can onto the Jack. The person whose hand gets there first wins the pile, adding it to the bottom of their own. If someone slaps the pile when there is no Jack, they have to pay a card out to each of the other players. Play continues until one player has won all the cards. This variation is fun, but can get a little rough. Referee!

WAR

This is another great introduction to playing cards for young children. It is a very simple game (after all, war is stupid), and a great one for children to play together: our kids can play War for an hour or more, replete with sound effects and their own extra-secret rules of engagement.

NUMBER OF PLAYERS	2
AGE	4 and up
YOU WILL NEED	One pack of cards
PLAYING TIME	20 to 40 minutes

OBJECT OF THE GAME
To win all the cards.

HOW TO PLAY
All cards are dealt out, so each player has 26 cards. Players place their stacks face down in front of them, and each turns up just the top card. The highest card wins, and the winner takes both his own and his opponent's cards and puts them face down at the bottom of his stack.

If the cards are of the same rank (we do not distinguish between suits in War), another card is turned up, and the higher card of this next pair wins all four cards (or, if the cards again rank the same, this process is repeated and the stacks grow).

This war of attrition continues, sometimes for a very long time, until one person has captured all of the cards.

STRIP JACK NAKED

Another great one for familiarising young players with suits and ranks; we loved this game as kids, and found great suspense in waiting for those powerful picture cards to appear. As with War, because this game is all in the luck of the deal, children and adults are on a completely level playing field.

NUMBER OF PLAYERS	2
AGE	4 and up
YOU WILL NEED	One pack of cards
PLAYING TIME	20 to 30 minutes

OBJECT OF THE GAME
To capture the whole pack.

HOW TO PLAY
Deal out all the cards as in Snap and War. Starting with the non-dealer, players take turns flipping over the top card of their stack and placing it on a common pile in the middle. If it is a number card, nothing happens and the

turn-taking continues. If a player turns over a King, Queen, Jack, or Ace, the other player has to pay them a 'tax' from their own stack, adding it to the central pile: one card for a Jack, two for a Queen, three for a King, and four for an Ace.

If the cards they use to pay the tax are only number cards, then the 'taxman' gets to claim the entire discard pile, placing it face down at the bottom of his own stack. However, if one of the cards used to pay the tax turns out to be an Ace or a picture card, payment stops immediately and the roles are reversed: the first player now has to pay out onto this card.

This taxing process can sometimes continue for a while, back and forth, until the cards used to pay up are only numbers, and the lucky player who played the last picture card or Ace wins the whole pile. He then starts the next round.

Play continues until one player has managed to Strip Jack Naked (that is, they win the whole pack).

MEMORY

You don't need a special boxed set of cards with pictures of Disney characters in order to play Memory, otherwise known as Concentration, Pelmanism, Pairs or, in Japan, *Shinkei-suijaku* (which, roughly translated, means 'nervous breakdown'). Parents should note that when your child hits nine or ten, no matter how hard you frown in concentration, they are going to beat you fair and square. Perhaps it could also be called 'Indignity'.

NUMBER OF PLAYERS	2 to 10
AGE	4 and up
YOU WILL NEED	A working memory and one full pack of cards, with or without a pair of Jokers
PLAYING TIME	30 minutes

OBJECT OF THE GAME
To collect the most pairs of cards of the same rank and colour (for example, Queen of Clubs and Queen of Spades; Seven of Hearts and Seven of Diamonds).

HOW TO PLAY
Cards need to be well shuffled and then laid out, one at a time, in six neat rows of nine cards each, with enough room left between cards so that they can be easily flipped over. (If you play without Jokers, two rows will have eight cards). Play starts left of the dealer and moves clockwise around the circle.

The first player starts by turning over any two cards so that everyone can see what they are. If they don't make a pair, the cards are turned face down again, and it is the next player's turn. If they do make a pair, the player gets to claim it and put it to one side, before turning over two more cards. Their turn continues until they have turned up two mismatched cards.

It is unusual to make pairs in the first few rounds but, as the game progresses and players begin to recall the locations of particular cards, play gets increasingly competitive.

When all pairs have been claimed, the game is over, and the person who collected the most cards wins. If there is a tie for first place, as sometimes happens, the two winners can go head to head in a mini-Memory game, using just five pairs from the pack.

VARIATIONS

For younger children, an easier version can be played in which pairs are matched only by rank but not colour (for example, a Jack of Diamonds could be matched with a Jack of Spades).

A harder version of Memory, sometimes called Spaghetti, involves laying cards face down in a completely random fashion (as if they have just been strewn across the floor), so that players have to build up a mental map of where the cards are, without relying on a traditional grid.

PIG

Also known as Donkey, this is an hilarious game, and thoroughly enjoyable for people of all ages. On a long caravanning trip, we played this often, and managed to pick up a plastic pink pig somewhere on our travels. This pig became part of the play, sitting on the table in front of whoever was last Pig. Obviously, a small plastic pig is entirely optional.

NUMBER OF PLAYERS	3 to 10
AGE	4 and up
YOU WILL NEED	Four equally ranking cards (for example, four ones) times the number of players. For example, for 4 players, you would need 16 cards comprising four sets of four cards of equal rank. We play with four aces, four twos, four threes, and four fours.
PLAYING TIME	5 to 10 mins

OBJECT OF THE GAME

To collect a full set of one rank in order to end the game — or to not be the last person who notices when someone else does!

HOW TO PLAY

Shuffle the small deck of cards well, then deal out four to each player, one at a time. At an agreed signal, and assuming no one has been dealt four of a kind, all players pass one card to their left and receive one card from their right. It works well to have the youngest player set the pace by saying 'pass' when they are ready to pass so that no one is left behind.

Play continues thus, until someone has collected four cards of equal rank (for example, four threes), at which time they silently place their finger on their nose. At varying speeds, other players will notice and silently follow suit. The last person to put their finger to their snout is Pig.

VARIATIONS

To play Tongue, play is identical, except that tongues are poked out rather than fingers put to noses.

To play Spoons, place one less spoons than there are players in the centre of the table, where everyone can easily reach them. The game proceeds identically to Pig, except that, instead of putting finger to nose, the first player to get a set of four equal-ranking cards surreptitiously takes a spoon and puts it in front of them. As the other players notice, they follow suit, and the last player left without a spoon loses. Never mind — play again.

OLD MAID

This game is like Pig's older cousin: a simple play of passing cards and making pairs, but with a few extra elements. Part of the fun of Old Maid is in watching fellow players try to keep a poker face when they are holding the Queen of Spades in their hand, and their sly attempts to pass it on.

NUMBER OF PLAYERS	3 to 6
AGE	5 and up
YOU WILL NEED	One pack of cards with all Queens removed, except the Queen of Spades
PLAYING TIME	20 minutes

OBJECT OF THE GAME
To not be left holding the Queen of Spades at the end of the game.

HOW TO PLAY
Deal out the entire pack, one at a time, clockwise around the circle. It doesn't matter if one or two players end up with an extra card. Players examine their hand and remove all pairs, placing them face up on the table in front of them. Pairs do not have to be the same colour, only the same rank. If a player has three of one rank, for example, three sixes, they only remove a pair and leave the third six in their hand.

The dealer then starts by fanning out his cards and offering them, face down, to the player on his left. This player has to draw out one mystery card and add it to her own hand. After looking again at her hand, she removes any new pair that might have been formed through the addition of the mystery card, and then offers her fanned-out cards, face down, to the player on her left.

Play continues around the circle, with players' hands shrinking as they remove their pairs to the table. Meanwhile, whoever is holding the Queen of Spades will be trying, in surreptitious (or comically obvious) ways, to have this card plucked from their hand by the player to their left: as the only Queen in the pack, the Queen of Spades can never be paired. Sometimes, the Queen of Spades moves round through all the players, and sometimes it gets stuck in one place.

When all the other cards have been paired up, the player who is left holding the Queen of Spades is the Old Maid and loses the game. (As the concept of the Old Maid is a dated one, it can make for some interesting table talk.)

VARIATIONS

A French version of this game, *Le Vieux Garçon*, or Old Boy, involves removing all Jacks except the Jack of Spades. Play is otherwise the same.

In the Philippines, they play an interesting variation where the dealer removes a single card at random, and without looking, so that nobody knows until the very end which card will be left over.

IT'S ALL IN THE SHUFFLE

There are heaps of ways to shuffle a deck of cards. Some people get pretty fancy about it. Below are six of the most popular shuffles to get you going. If you are left-handed, reverse the instructions accordingly. And if you really want to impress, try the Hindu Shuffle with your eyes closed and while counting backwards in sevens from ninety-eight. Once you've mastered this, try the Riffle Shuffle using your feet. (If you actually get anywhere with this, please get in touch; we'd like to meet you.)

THE WASH SHUFFLE

This is a popular method with children, also known as the Scramble or Beginner Shuffle. Cards are spread out face down on the table and thoroughly mixed up, sans detergent, before being driven back together and into a stack.

THE PILE SHUFFLE

Another good one for children whose hands aren't big enough to manage the trickier shuffles. Simply deal cards out into any number of small piles, which are then stacked on top of one another in a random order, ensuring cards that were beside one another are now separated. Repeat several times.

THE OVERHAND SHUFFLE

This is the standard lazy shuffle used by most people on most occasions, also called the Stripping Shuffle or the Slide Shuffle. You could master this and go no further. Hold the cards lightly in your left hand, with your fingers resting against the back of the deck. Use your right hand to lift a stack of cards from the back of the deck, and then hold them above the other stack. With your right thumb, release the first few cards onto the front of the pack. Move forward, let go of the next few. Repeat this action several times before selecting another stack from the back. All you are doing is moving small groups of cards from one side of the deck to the other. Repeat process up to ten times.

OVERHAND

THE WEAVE SHUFFLE

This is another simple shuffle, and a good one for those who haven't yet mastered the Riffle. Divide the cards into two rough halves. Hold one half very loosely in the left hand, as in the Overhand, and hold the other half, loosely, directly above. With a gentle sawing action (if you're too rough, you'll damage the cards), weave the two halves together until they are overlapping by a few centimetres, then bend the cards with the palm of the left hand to release the pressure, allowing the two halves to cascade together. (If you can't get the cascade happening, just push the packets together.) Square off the pack. Repeat at least three times.

WEAVE

THE RIFFLE SHUFFLE

Also called the Dovetail Shuffle, this is easy, once you get the hang of it, and very efficient. Divide the pack into two rough halves, and put them each face down, bringing them together at the corners. While holding down each half with your fingers, use your thumbs to bend up just the corners, sliding the two portions closer together until they interlock. Let the cards riffle downwards, interleaving as they go. Loosen your fingers and slide the two halves together. Square off the pack. Repeat three times.

RIFFLE

THE HINDU SHUFFLE

Also called the Kenchi (Hindi for 'scissors'), the Hindu Shuffle is the most common in Asia, and is a smooth, impressive shuffle. The more you practise, the faster you get. Hold the deck firmly by the end, with your left thumb and middle finger, index finger resting on top. The right hand comes underneath and, using your right thumb and middle finger, lightly slides a small packet of cards off the top of the deck. These fall on the palm of the right hand, but are trapped in place by the index finger. Right hand goes beneath again, and the action is repeated ten times or more, until the last few cards slide onto the top of the deck held in your right hand. Square off the pack. Repeat three times.

HINDU

CRAZY EIGHTS

Otherwise known as Wild Eights or Swedish Rummy, Crazy Eights is very similar to the trademarked Uno, but it uses a normal deck of cards. It's another good one for familiarising kids with suits and ranks. There is lots of luck involved, but this is also a game of skill. Playing this, children will start to learn how to make decisions about which cards to keep and which to discard, and about when to use wild cards and when to hold on to them.

NUMBER OF PLAYERS	2 to 8
AGE	5 and up
YOU WILL NEED	For 2 to 5 players, one pack of cards; for 6 or more players, two packs shuffled together; paper and pencil for scoring
PLAYING TIME	20 to 30 minutes

OBJECT OF THE GAME
To discard all of the cards in your hand.

HOW TO PLAY
Deal seven cards each for a two-player game; for anything above, you will need five cards apiece. The rest of the pack goes face down in the centre of the table to form the stock, with the top card turned over beside the pile, face up, to start the discard pile. If the first card turned up is an eight, it must be buried in the middle of the pack and a new card turned over.

The player to the left of the dealer starts by placing a card onto the discard pile. The card placed must match the face-up card in either suit or rank. For example, if a Five of Hearts has been turned up, the first player can play either another five or another heart. The only exception is when a player has an eight, which is the wild card. An eight can be played at any time and, when it is used, the player gets to nominate a suit (not a rank) for continuing play. They might say 'diamonds', for example, if they have a lot of diamonds in their hand.

If a player doesn't have a card that matches the face-up card in suit or rank, or an eight, they pick up a card from the stock, and continue to do so until they can play their turn. Importantly, players can also choose to pick up from the stock even when they are able to play. This can be important when trying to prevent someone else from winning.

Play continues clockwise around the table until someone wins the game by managing to discard all of their cards.

If you choose to score, cards left in the hands of the losing players at the end of a game are added up and allocated to the winner according to the following values: an eight is worth 50, picture cards are worth ten, an Ace is worth one, and the rest are scored at face value. Hence, only the winner of a hand will record a score. To make an evening of it, play until someone reaches one hundred and fifty.

GO FISH

Another classic game for young card sharks that requires players to keep track of who is fishing for which cards, so they can beat them to the catch.

NUMBER OF PLAYERS	2 to 6
AGE	6 and up
YOU WILL NEED	One pack of cards
PLAYING TIME	20 to 30 minutes

OBJECT OF THE GAME

To collect the most sets of four of the same rank (for example, four sevens).

HOW TO PLAY

For two or three players, seven cards are dealt to each player. For four to six players, just five cards are dealt to each. The remaining cards are placed face down in the middle of the table to form the stock.

Players examine their hand, and then the person to the left of the dealer starts play. This person addresses by name any other player in the game, asking them if they have cards of a particular rank. For example, 'Mary, do you have any sevens?' A player can only ask this if they are holding at least one seven in their own hand. If the person who has been addressed is able to oblige, they must do so, handing over as many sevens as they have in their hand. The first player then gets to ask again, either for a card of the same rank or a different one, and from the same player or another one. As long as his run of luck continues, he keeps fishing until he asks a particular player for something which they don't have. When that happens, the player will reply, 'Go fish!' When this happens, often at the first request, the player asking has to pick up the top card from the stock, and play passes to his left.

As the game progresses, players get to know what cards other players are trying to collect, and so are in a position to take these off them when it is their turn to fish. When players have gathered all four cards of one rank, to form a full set, they put this face up on the table in front of them. Note: if, when told to 'go fish', a player picks up from the stock a card that completes a set in their hand, their turn continues. Also, if a player runs out of cards while there is still a stockpile, they pick up a single card from the stock and continue playing.

The fishing trip ends when all 13 sets have been laid down in front of the players. The winner is the player with the biggest catch.

QUEEN OF HEARTS JAM TART

As children, we relished our visits to Great-Uncle Allan and Great-Aunty Pat, who lived in an old gold-mining area not far from the city of Ballarat. We would stay in the vacant workman's cottage on their property, and every night, after dinner, we'd put on cardigans, grab torches, and head up the hill to the big house. Cards nights at the big house had a lot going for them: a warm, bright kitchen with a good-sized table for games; three card-tricking second cousins; and fabulous home-baked treats, including sponge cake, jam tart, biscuits, and scones, served with the freshest possible cream from their cows, Strawberry and Daisy. We played Cheat and ate till we could eat no more.

Snacks at cards nights are essential: a packet of shortbread or a bowl of olives and some cheese and crackers are fine. But, if you can find the time, try this recipe for a delicious jam and almond tart to serve with a family-sized pot of tea (see p. 220 for how to make the perfect pot). Great-Aunty Pat, this one's for you.

FOR THE PASTRY, YOU WILL NEED:
1 cup of plain flour, a pinch of salt,
1 tablespoon of sugar; ½ teaspoon of
lemon zest, 125g of butter at room
temperature, 1 tablespoon of water,
a splash of vanilla essence.

FOR THE FILLING, YOU WILL NEED:
½ cup ground almonds, ⅓ of a cup of sugar, pinch of salt, 2 eggs,
generous splash of vanilla essence, ½ of a cup of butter at room
temperature, 2 tablespoons of plain flour, ½ teaspoon of baking
powder, 4 tablespoons of jam of choice (preferably not too sweet),
½ cup of slivered almonds, icing sugar to sprinkle.

TO MAKE PASTRY SHELL:
Rub butter into flour with salt, sugar, and zest until you have a coarse
meal. Add water and vanilla, and mix lightly until you have formed
a ball of dough. (This can all be done in the food processor.) Wrap
dough in plastic, and rest it for 30 minutes in the fridge.

Grease a 23cm flan tin with a removable bottom. Because the
dough is so buttery, use your hands to spread the pastry over the base
and up the sides, to a centimetre or two above the rim (it will shrink
during baking). Preheat oven to 200°C. Freeze for another 30 minutes,
or until dough is firm. Partially bake shell in lower part of oven for
about ten minutes, checking halfway to pierce air bubbles that may
have formed. Remove when just golden, and allow to cool.

TO FILL TART:
Turn oven down to 190°C. Blend ground almonds, sugar, salt, eggs,
and vanilla. Add butter, flour, and baking powder, and blend or beat
until smooth-ish. Spread thick layer of jam onto tart shell, then cover
with almond mixture. Scatter slivered almonds on top, and bake for 30
minutes, or until surface is firm and golden brown. Remove from oven
and allow to cool before dusting with icing sugar.

Serve in wedges, with or without big dollops of cream.

CUCKOO

Also known as Ranter Go Round, Cuckoo is quick and fun, perfect for a bit of winding down after school and before homework. We use nuts or breakfast cereal for a stake, which we put in a small bowl in the middle of the table for the victor to gobble up.

NUMBER OF PLAYERS	3 or more
AGE	7 and up
YOU WILL NEED	One pack of cards and something small, and preferably edible, to use as a stake
PLAYING TIME	3 to 5 minutes per hand

OBJECT OF THE GAME
To not be left with the lowest card (suits are not important).

HOW TO PLAY
Players start out with three lives. One card is dealt to each player, all of whom look at their cards. The player to the left of the dealer starts by deciding whether or not to exchange his card with the person to his left, in the hope of getting a higher card. If he is happy with the card he has, he can keep it. If he chooses to exchange it, his neighbour has no choice but to swap, although his new card may turn out, of course, to be lower in value than the one being exchanged. The only circumstance in which a player can refuse to swap their card with the person to their right is if they have a King, in which case they put it down in front of them, face up, at the beginning of the game. In this instance, the player to their right has no choice but to keep their card.

Play passes clockwise around the circle with each player deciding whether or not to swap their card with the player to their left. When it reaches the dealer's turn, the dealer can either keep her card or exchange it with the one on top of the remaining stock; though, again, if this turns out to be a King, she has to stick with the original card.

After everyone has had one opportunity to exchange, players reveal their cards, and the person with the lowest card loses a life. If there is a tie for lowest place, both players lose lives.

The person to the left of the dealer now deals the next round, and play continues thus. When a player has lost all of their lives, they are out of the game, and the last player left in the game at the end wins the stake. Gobble gobble.

GOLF

Sometimes called Polish Poker or Turtle, Golf is a fabulous game from which the best-selling Rat-a-Tat Cat card game was derived. As in the sport golf, the aim is to score as little as possible. This is another great one for exercising your memory, as you need to keep track of which cards are in which face-down positions.

NUMBER OF PLAYERS	2 to 6
AGE	7 and up
YOU WILL NEED	One pack of cards
PLAYING TIME	5 to 10 minutes per 'hole'

OBJECT OF THE GAME
To achieve the lowest score with your cards.

HOW TO PLAY
Each player is dealt four cards, one at a time, which are placed face down in a square grid (two by two) in front of them. The rest of the cards form a stockpile in the centre of the table, with the top card turned over, face up, to start the discard pile. Before play begins, all players sneak a peek at the two bottom cards in their square, not letting anyone else see. After this, the cards in the square are not seen again until either discarded during play or scored at the end.

The player to the left of the dealer starts by drawing one card from the stockpile or taking the top card from the discard pile. This card can be used to replace an unwanted card in the square in front of him, with the unwanted card then discarded, face up, onto the discard pile. However, if a card is picked up from the stock that the player doesn't want to keep, this is placed directly onto the discard pile.

173

Play proceeds clockwise around the circle, with players at each turn drawing one card from either the stock or discard pile and deciding whether to use it to replace a face-down card. Players try to lower the value of their face-down cards both by keeping low cards and also by making pairs that cancel themselves out to equal zero (see scoring, below). Because the bottom two cards of the square have been seen, it is fairly straightforward deciding whether or not to replace them with any given card. With the top two cards, however, you have to take a punt. Bear in mind that, once a card has been replaced, you still need to remember what and where it is, so as to keep lowering your overall score as the game progresses. This is not as easy as it sounds.

When a player thinks they have a good chance of achieving the lowest score, they knock on their next turn, to indicate that they are going out, after picking up a card and before discarding their last one. Each of the other players is then allowed one more turn before the game ends.

Cards are turned face up, and scored as follows: number cards are scored at face value, with Ace being counted as one. Jacks and Queens score ten points. Kings score zero, so they are the most sought-after cards in the pack. Also, together, any pair of cards of equal rank (for example, two nines) score zero. The player with the lowest score wins the round.

Traditionally, nine games are played, as in nine-hole golf, and the person with the lowest cumulative score at the end wins the day on the green. Or, if you want to go all out, make it an 18-hole game.

VARIATIONS

There are several variations to the rules of Golf that can make it easier for younger players:

1. Peek at all four cards at the beginning, rather than just the bottom two.
2. Only peek at the bottom two, but do so at any time during the game.
3. To make it really easy, hold all four cards in your hand, eliminating any need to remember what and where they are.

CHEAT

Otherwise known as I Doubt It, this is a wonderful game, and a favourite of just about every child who has ever played it. It requires mathematical skills, daring, and the ability to keep a straight face. Play it, love it, and don't worry too much that you are encouraging your children to tell bald-faced lies.

NUMBER OF PLAYERS	3 to 8
AGE	8 and up
YOU WILL NEED	One pack of cards for 3 to 4 players, or two packs shuffled together for 5 or more
PLAYING TIME	20 to 30 minutes

OBJECT OF THE GAME
To be the first person to discard all of the cards in your hand.

HOW TO PLAY
All the cards are dealt out one at a time, moving clockwise around the table. After hands have been examined, the player to the left of the dealer starts by putting up to four cards face down in the middle of the table, announcing aloud what they are, for example, 'four fives'. (When playing with two packs, this could be up to eight cards.) In theory, all cards put down on a turn have to be of the same rank; in practice, the point is to get rid of your cards as fast as you can by cheating. You may say 'four fives' while actually putting down two sevens and two twos, for example.

If the first player goes unchallenged, the second player now places up to four cards face down on top of the pile. These have to be, in theory, cards of the rank above or below the previous one: so, if fives were played previously, the next player can put down fours or sixes. Of course, they might really put down the cards that they declare, or they might not. If a player has no cards of the ranks above or below, they are not permitted to miss their turn but have to cheat and put something down anyway.

It quickly becomes obvious that someone is cheating: how can two people have put down three Jacks each? But who is the cheat? (Again, if you are playing with two packs, there will be eight cards of each rank to account for.) If a player feels reasonably confident that another player has cheated on their turn, they call 'Cheat!' or 'I doubt it!' at which point the topmost suspect cards are turned over. If found guilty, the cheat has to pick up the entire pile of discarded cards and add it to their hand; however, if the player is innocent, their accuser has to pick up the cards. Hence, players are taking a risk not only by cheating but also by challenging. Whoever has picked up the discard pile restarts the game with any rank they choose.

The faster you play Cheat, the better the game is; hesitating only makes you look guilty. The first player who manages to discard all of their cards — usually the best cheat — wins.

VARIATIONS

To play a simpler version of this game, cards can be announced in any order and don't have to be the rank above or below the previous call.

To play a more difficult game, the next rank called must always be one higher than the last, so play starts at Ace, then moves upwards through the ranks to King, then starts again at Ace.

SEVENS

This one was taught to us by a visiting English uncle, and we have been playing it ever since. Variously called Fan Tan, Parliament, and Card Dominoes, Sevens is a strategic game that involves obstructing the play of others as well as trying to get ahead yourself.

NUMBER OF PLAYERS	3 to 8
AGES	8 and up
YOU WILL NEED	One pack of cards
PLAYING TIME	15 to 20 mins

OBJECT OF THE GAME

To be the first to get rid of all the cards in your hand.

HOW TO PLAY

Cards are distributed one at a time, clockwise around the table, until all cards have been dealt. It doesn't matter if some players get an extra card. Once players have examined their hands and arranged them into suits, the person holding the Seven of Hearts starts by placing it in the centre of the table. Play now moves to the left of this person, with the next player either placing a seven of a different suit down next to the Seven of Hearts; or putting an Eight of Hearts above the Seven of Hearts, or a Six of Hearts below: that is, a card in the same suit and in sequence. If they cannot make any of these three moves, they must pass, and play moves to their left.

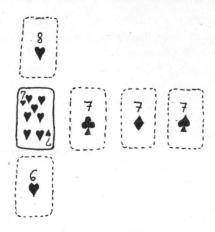

From hereon, players build either up or down in sequence from the sevens on the table, bearing in mind that a seven has to be the first card put down for each suit. Stacks of cards gradually accumulate above and below each seven in the row. Where it becomes strategic is in players' attempts to block one another. For example, a player holding a Seven of Clubs may choose to hold it back and keep adding to other suits, thereby not allowing anyone else to get rid of their Clubs. Similarly, they might refrain from putting down the Ten of Hearts, for example, so the stack can move no further up. However, if they can, players *must* put down a card on each turn.

The winner is the first person to put down all their cards.

RACING DEMON

As the name suggests, this is a race, so you can forget right now about manners and turn-taking. It is, however, great for your sequencing, concentration, and fine motor skills … yes, kids are particularly good at it. Also known (aptly) as Pounce, this fast-moving game of group Patience looks complicated at first, but once you get the hang of it you'll be flying along.

NUMBER OF PLAYERS	2 to 10
AGE	9 and up
YOU WILL NEED	One pack of cards for each player, each pack with a different pattern on the back; paper and pencil for scoring
PLAYING TIME	10 minutes

OBJECT OF THE GAME

To achieve the highest score by using up all the cards in your pile and by putting the most cards on the centre stacks.

HOW TO PLAY

Each player, using his own pack of cards, deals himself a pile of 13 cards face up. For simplicity's sake, we'll call this the Pile. Four more cards — the line-up cards — are laid out in a row, face up, above the Pile, while the rest of the stock is held in the hand to be used in play.

At the word 'go', the race begins. First off, any player who has turned up an Ace — from the line-up cards or from the Pile — moves it to the common space in the middle of the table, where everyone can play on it (these are the centre stacks). Whenever Aces appear during the game, they are put straight in the middle to form new centre stacks. Cards on the centre stacks are built up sequentially, from Ace through to King, in the same suit; that is, hearts can only go on hearts, clubs on clubs, etc. When a player puts a final King onto a centre stack, he gets to take that stack and put it to one side, where it will add to his score later.

Each player now does everything they can to get rid of their Pile, and to get as many cards as possible onto the centre stacks. When two players both want to put the same card onto a centre stack, it is a race to see who gets there first. Cards can be added to the centre stacks from the top of the player's Pile, from the line-up cards, or from the stock in the player's hand, which is sifted through three cards at a time, as in classic Patience. Whenever a card is moved from your line-up to a centre stack, it is replaced from the Pile.

As well as building on the centre stacks, you reduce your Pile by 'laddering'. This is where you build on to your four line-up cards; but, instead of staying in suit and going upwards, as with the centre stacks, the ladders go down (for example: six, five, four, three) and alternate between red and black cards — again, as in classic Patience. You can ladder using cards from your Pile, the stock, and also other cards in the line-up that you then replace from the Pile, all of which is helping to shrink the Pile and get you closer to the finishing line.

The first player to get rid of all the cards in their Pile (but not the line-up cards or the stock) shouts 'Out!' — usually quite loudly — and play stops immediately. Do not pack up or move any cards yet, because they are all needed in scoring.

Scoring is as follows, and has to be done in a certain sequence: the first person to get rid of their Pile gets ten bonus points straight up. Any player who has put aside a centre stack (having added the King) gets five points for each stack. All players who didn't finish their Piles now count the remaining cards (only the number of cards, the values don't matter) and make a record of this number — it will be subtracted from the rest of their score.

All the centre stacks that were finished and removed are now put back in the middle, face down, alongside the half-done stacks, which are now also turned over to be face down. The remainder of the players' stocks, Piles, and line-up cards are pushed to one side. Sifting through the centre stacks, each player now collects all of their own cards (according to the pattern of their deck) and adds them up. Each card is one point. From this number, they subtract the number of cards they had remaining in their Pile, and add relevant bonus points for completing stacks with Kings, and/or for finishing their Pile first. (Don't be alarmed if your score is negative; it happens.)

The Racing Demon is the person with the highest score. If you want to keep going, as we suspect you will, play until someone reaches 100 (about four or five games).

WHIST

This well-loved game can be traced back to the early 16th century, and was extremely popular in the parlours of the Victorian era. It is the forerunner to the more elaborate game of Bridge, which appeared at the end of the 19th century. Presented in its simplest form here, Whist is a good game for introducing older children to the concepts of tricks and trumps, counting cards, and the fun of playing with a partner.

NUMBER OF PLAYERS	4, in partnerships
AGE	9 and up
YOU WILL NEED	One pack of cards; paper and pencil for scoring. Note: Ace is high.
PLAYING TIME	10 minutes per hand

OBJECT OF THE GAME
To win the most tricks.

HOW TO PLAY
You play with a partner in this game, and adults with children works well. Partners sit opposite one another. Starting from the left, the dealer deals out all the cards, face down, one at a time. The very last card for the dealer's hand is turned face up, and whatever suit it is will be the trump suit for the game; that is, cards in this suit will be more powerful than any other card in

the pack. The dealer adds this card to her hand. Each player should have 13 cards each.

The person to the left of the dealer now leads, by putting down any card of their choice. Each person thereafter has to follow suit if they can; if they cannot, they are permitted to play any other card, including a trump. When each person has played one card, this constitutes a trick: that is, four cards. Whoever has won the trick takes it and puts it to one side (one person from each partnership will generally keep their tricks together).

A trick containing a trump will always be won by the person who has played the highest trump. So, if, for example, hearts are trumps, a Two of Hearts will beat the King of Clubs. A trick not containing any trumps is won by the player of the highest card of the suit led: that is, the first card in the trick. The winner of each trick always leads the next.

While the rules of Whist are fairly straightforward, it is a strategic game. Players need to keep track of what cards have already been played, which players have which suits, and how best to work with their partner.

When all the cards have been played, the tricks in each partnership are added up, and one game point is awarded for each trick after the first six. For the next hand, the deal passes to the player to the left of the first dealer and, again, the last card dealt will determine trumps for the new hand. The first side to reach seven points wins the game.

This is a Saturday-night, after-dinner game. Bake a jam tart for this one.

The evening glided swiftly away, in these cheerful recreations;
and when the substantial though homely supper had been despatched,
and the little party formed a social circle round the fire, Mr Pickwick thought
he had never felt so happy in his life, and at no time so much disposed
to enjoy, and make the most of, the passing moment.
— An evening of Whist, as described by Charles Dickens
in *The Pickwick Papers*

BLACK LADY

Also known as Hearts or Black Maria, this is another trick-taking game. This time, the aim is to avoid scoring points: the winner is the loser. Enjoy!

NUMBER OF PLAYERS	3 to 7
AGE	9 and up
YOU WILL NEED	Paper and pencil for scoring; one pack of cards. Depending on the number of players, discard twos as follows, to make the pack divide up evenly: remove one two for three players, none for four, two twos for five players, none for six, and three twos for seven players (leaving in the Two of Hearts). Note: Ace is high.
PLAYING TIME	10 minutes per hand

OBJECT OF THE GAME
To score the fewest number of points by taking the fewest tricks with hearts or the Queen of Spades in them.

HOW TO PLAY
The pack is dealt out evenly to players, one at a time. Before play begins, players look at their hands and choose three cards to pass to the player on their right. (The idea is to pass on high-scoring cards.)

The player to the left of the dealer starts, leading with any card they wish. All players are compelled to follow suit, if they can, and the player of the highest card takes the trick (ouch!), then leads the next. There are no trumps in Black Lady, so the highest card in the suit led always wins the trick. Because the aim is to win as few tricks as possible that contain hearts or the Queen of Spades, it is a good opportunity to discard these troublesome cards, if you are unable to follow suit on any trick.

At the end of each hand, players look at the tricks they have won, and add up their score as follows: all hearts are worth one point, and the Black Lady (Queen of Spades) is worth thirteen. When the first player reaches 50 points, thereby losing, the game ends and the player with the lowest score wins.

PONTOON

Pontoon, also called 21, is a gambling game, a version of which (Blackjack) is played in casinos the world over. Apparently, it was the game of choice among soldiers in the First World War trenches. As kids, we used to bet with matchsticks, but pretty much anything, including small change, buttons, or sweets, will do. We have simplified betting and scoring conventions here for family use.

NUMBER OF PLAYERS	2 to 10
AGES	9 and up
YOU WILL NEED	One pack of cards, and something small and numerous, such as matchsticks, to use for betting. Note: the Ace can be counted as either 1 or 11.
PLAYING TIME	5 mins per hand

OBJECT OF THE GAME

To have cards that add up to a higher value than the dealer's but do not exceed 21 (a 'pontoon').

HOW TO PLAY

Everyone starts with an equal number of matchsticks or other betting tokens; somewhere between ten and 20 is good. Before the game begins, a Joker is placed, face up, at the bottom of the pack, to mark the end of the shuffled cards. After each hand, cards are put to the bottom of the pack, but the deck is not reshuffled until the Joker is reached.

The dealer gives everyone one card, face down, starting from her left and dealing herself last. After looking at this card, each player has the option of placing a bet or staying out of the game for that round. It is good to agree at the beginning on minimum and maximum bets: nothing less than one matchstick and nothing more than three works well. The dealer lays down her bet last. In this game, you are not betting against other players, only against the dealer.

The dealer than deals each player, including herself, a second card, face down. The two cards are examined. A 'natural pontoon' is two cards that add up to 21; that is, an Ace with a picture card or a ten.

An Ace can be counted as either one or 11; picture cards are ten; and number cards are face value.

If any player has a natural pontoon after the second card is dealt, he must reveal it straight away and will be paid out double his bet by the dealer, unless the dealer also has a natural pontoon. (If a player's cards are equal to the dealer's, the dealer always wins.) If the dealer has a natural pontoon, the round is over then and there, and each player must pay the dealer double the amount of her bet.

If the dealer does not have a natural pontoon (and once any other player has revealed a natural pontoon and been paid out) the dealer starts with the player at her left, and asks if they would like another card. The player is dealt as many cards as they request, one at a time, until they either 'bust' (go over 21), and lose their stake to the dealer, or 'stick', deciding to hold on to their cards and get no more.

When all players have either bust or stuck, the dealer turns over her cards, face up and, with everyone watching, deals herself as many cards as she wants, with the aim of reaching 21, or as close to as she dares. If the dealer busts, she has to pay out the equivalent of their bets to all players who have stuck, but she still gets to keep the matches of players who have also bust. If the dealer sticks, the other players now reveal their cards. The dealer pays out players with a higher total who stuck, and collects from those with the same or a lower total who stuck.

The next round can now commence, with the role of dealer rotating clockwise around the circle to even up any advantage.

Players are out of the game when they run out of matches (or buttons or whatever), and a good session of Pontoon continues until one player has won the lot.

GIN RUMMY

This is the most popular of all the rummies, invented in a club in New York in 1909. It's a game for adults and older children, who, once initiated, will pester you for it for evermore. We often play it when the kids have gone to bed — if they knew, they'd be horrified.

NUMBER OF PLAYERS	2
AGE	10 and up
YOU WILL NEED	One pack of cards; paper and pencil for scoring
PLAYING TIME	10 to 15 minutes per hand

OBJECT OF THE GAME
To score the most points by having the fewest unmatched cards in your hand when the game ends.

HOW TO PLAY
Players are dealt ten cards each, with the remaining cards forming the stock in the middle of the table. Turn over the top card of the stock, and put it down beside the stockpile, to make the discard pile.

The non-dealer starts by either taking a card from the stock or picking up the top card of the discard pile and adding that card to her hand. She then has to discard a card, so that the cards in her hand always number ten. From hereon, players take it in turns to pick up from the stock or the discard pile and to then discard a card, as they try to build up matched sets in their hands. A matched set is three or four cards of the same rank (for example, three sevens), or three or more cards in sequence in the same suit (for example, Three of Hearts, Four of Hearts, Five of Hearts).

As the game progresses, the matched sets in your hand are constantly changing and evolving, with difficult decisions along the way about which cards to keep and which to discard. All matched sets are held, concealed, in the hand until one of the players brings the game to an end by 'knocking'. You knock when it is your turn, to indicate the game's over, in between drawing a card and laying down your final card, face down, on the discard pile. You can only knock when the value of your unmatched cards is ten points or fewer. If you knock when all ten of your cards are in matched sets, this is called a 'gin hand'. A gin hand might look like this: Three of Spades, Three of Clubs, Three of Hearts; Seven of Hearts, Eight of Hearts, Nine of Hearts, Ten of Hearts; Ace of Diamonds, Two of Diamonds, Three of Diamonds.

If the knocker doesn't have a 'gin hand', he lays his cards, face up, in matched sets and unmatched cards. The opponent is then entitled to add any of his own unmatched cards to the knocker's matched sets. In the case of a gin hand, the opponent is not permitted to add any cards.

Scoring is as follows:

If you knock with a gin hand, you score a 25-point bonus as well as the total value of any unmatched cards in your opponent's hand. An Ace is worth one point; picture cards are worth ten points; and number cards are scored at face value. If you knock without a gin hand, after the opponent has added any unmatched cards to the knocker's matched sets, the value of the unmatched cards in each hand is added up. If the opponent's count is higher than the knocker's, the knocker is awarded the difference. However, if the opponent has the same or a lower score, she gets the difference plus a 25-point bonus for undercutting the knocker.

Gin Rummy is intended to be played as a game with a running total scored from hand to hand. The winner of each hand deals the next, and the first player to reach 100 points wins the overall game (we find it hard to stop, so we usually go to one hundred and fifty).

GAMES OF DICE

The dice of Zeus fall ever luckily.
— Sophocles

Dice have been around almost as long as people, and are believed to have originated independently in several ancient cultures, rather than in one place. The earliest 'dice' were fruit stones, sea shells, and pebbles, thrown by witchdoctors and shamans to divine the future. You might consider this the next time you casually toss your apricot pit onto the compost heap. But the first cubical dice, used by the Greeks and Romans, were sheep's anklebones (known colloquially as 'knucklebones'), with each side of the bone allocated a different value. The Greeks and Romans were great gamblers, and the goddess Fortuna, daughter of Zeus, was said to determine the outcome of a roll.

Our present-day six-sided cubical die appeared around 600 BC, and has changed little since, though dice are now made from cellulose acetate, rather than the more earthy bone and clay. It's easy to see why dice have maintained their popularity through the millennia: they are great fun to play with. Highly portable, great for mental arithmetic, a bunch of dice make a very satisfying clickety click as they jumble together in your palm and then scatter across the table.

Some people use a cup for shaking their dice; we prefer two hands cupped together, but please yourselves. If you don't own a full set of dice, gather them together from old boxed games, or look underneath that armchair you haven't moved in years. A handful of big and small, light and heavy, yellowing and white makes a great set of playing dice.

We don't recommend you bet your house on the roll of the die; yet, surely it's their gambling origins that give dice games that extra frisson of excitement. Does someone in your family have the luck of Zeus? Do patterns emerge? How do you choose to explain them? And why is that little one with red spots always coming up a six? Could it be loaded?

WHO GETS FIRST ROLL?

In our family, it's the youngest who goes first (random luck-of-birth order). If you want to make it fairer, each player rolls a die once, and the person with the highest throw starts, with play continuing clockwise. If two or more players tie on this first roll, those players roll again.

BEETLE

This is a lovely game for very young children, although older kids enjoy it, too. While Beetle is a game of pure chance, it does provide an opportunity to show off your drawing skills.

NUMBER OF PLAYERS	2 to 6
AGE	3 and up
YOU WILL NEED	One die, and a piece of paper and a pencil (or pen, crayons, coloured pencils) for each player
PLAYING TIME	20 minutes

OBJECT OF THE GAME

To be the first player to finish drawing your beetle.

HOW TO PLAY

The first player rolls the die and, depending on whether they get a one, they either get to start drawing their beetle or wait until their next turn. Either way, each player has just one roll before passing the die to their left.

The beetle comprises 12 body parts: body, head, two feelers, two eyes, and six legs. Only one part can be drawn on a single successful roll of the die. The body parts correspond to the following dice values:

- One for the body
- Two for the head
- Three for each eye
- Four for each feeler
- Five or six for each leg

To start their beetle, players have to roll a one for the body before they are permitted to add anything else; sometimes, this takes a few goes. Once you have a body, you can start adding legs but, again, eyes or feelers can't go on until you've rolled a two for the head.

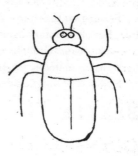

Play continues around the circle until the game ends, when the first beetle has been completed and its artist is declared winner. (Colour beetles in, draw patterns on their backs, give them names and stick 'em on the fridge.)

PIG DICE

Also known as Greedy Pig, this is a simple, fast game of jeopardy. Maths teachers often use it to teach the concept of probability. Because the game involves players deciding when to bank their scores, or when to keep going at the risk of losing it all, it separates the family into the risk-takers and the plodders. Interesting …

NUMBER OF PLAYERS	2 to 10
AGE	4 and up
YOU WILL NEED	One die, and paper and pencil for scoring
PLAYING TIME	20 minutes

OBJECT OF THE GAME
To be the first player to reach 50 points.

HOW TO PLAY
The first player starts by rolling the die. If a two, three, four, five, or six is rolled, points are earned according to the face value of the die. The player then chooses to either bank the score or roll again. On a single turn, the die can be rolled an indefinite number of times, with the player adding points as they go along. However, if a one is rolled, the turn ends, and all accumulated

points are wiped out.

For example, Mary rolls a four and decides to continue. She then rolls five, four, six, and then one. She earns zero points. Dave rolls a five, and decides to continue. He then rolls two, three, five, and six and decides to bank his score of twenty-one.

Play passes to the left and continues until the winner has reached 50 points — or 100, for a longer game.

DROP DEAD

This is another game of sheer luck, so young and old have an equal chance of winning. If you want to spice it up, you can start with a wager: a handful of choc drops does nicely. Another fantastic one for mental arithmetic.

NUMBER OF PLAYERS	2 to 10
AGE	4 and up
YOU WILL NEED	Five dice; paper and pencil for scoring; and something to bet with, if you are so inclined
PLAYING TIME	20 minutes

OBJECT OF THE GAME
To be the first player to reach 50 points, or the person with the highest score after an agreed number of rounds.

HOW TO PLAY
Roll the dice to decide who will start. If you want to, place a wager at the centre of the table for the winner to scoop. The first player then throws all five dice. If the dice rolled include a two or five, these are set to one side, and the remaining dice are rolled again. If, however, none of the dice are a two or five, the face values of all the dice are added up, and then all are rolled again. The player continues to roll the dice, setting aside twos and fives, and not earning points on rolls where these numbers appear. Dice are gradually reduced until the last die is a two or five. This is when you 'drop dead' and the turn is over, with play moving to the left. Hence, it is possible to score

zero on your turn, if on each roll you get a two or a five. Alternatively, your score might reach as high as 50 in one turn.

For example, say Peter rolls first a four, three, five, one, one. He scores no points, puts the five to one side, and rolls again. Next time, he rolls six, one, four, four. He scores 15 points and rolls all the dice again. Next time, he rolls two, three, five, six, and scores no points, setting five and two aside. On his fourth roll, he gets a six and a one: seven points. On his fifth roll, Peter rolls five and three. He scores nil, and sets the five aside. On his sixth roll, he gets a four — four more points. On his seventh roll, he gets a two and drops dead: his turn is over. Altogether, he has scored 26 points — not bad.

Play continues around the circle until someone has reached 50 points, or you have completed a previously agreed number of rounds. Winner gets the choc drops.

SHIP, CAPTAIN, AND CREW

Also known as Ship of Fools, this is a lovely game that beautifully captures children's imaginations (although it did start out as a Navy drinking game). Particular dice are said to represent a ship, captain, crew, and cargo. When we play, a running story is always told about ships alone at sea without their captains, captains without their ships, giant waves, whales, and floating cargo.

NUMBER OF PLAYERS	2 to 10
AGE	4 and up
YOU WILL NEED	Five dice, and paper and pencil for scoring
PLAYING TIME	20 to 30 minutes

OBJECT OF THE GAME
To be either the first player to reach 50 points or the player with the highest score at the end of an agreed number of rounds.

HOW TO PLAY

The first player rolls all five dice, with the aim of capturing a ship (six), then a captain (five), and then crew (four). They have to be captured in this order because, obviously, you cannot have a captain without a ship, and so on. Hence, if you have rolled a five and four but no six, you will have to roll all the dice again. In a turn, a player has three rolls of the dice, removing the ship (six), captain (five), and crew (four) as they go. If, at the end of three goes, the player has managed to secure all three, the remaining dice (the cargo) are added together to form the score. If the player assembles the ship, captain, and crew by the first or second roll, she can choose between keeping the cargo or re-rolling just those two dice to try to get a higher score. Note that both remaining dice must be rolled, not just one. If, however, she has been unsuccessful at assembling the special numbers by the end of her three rolls, she scores no cargo points at all.

The winner is the first person to reach 50 points, or the player with the highest score after an agreed number of rounds.

VARIATION

If you want to add another element, you can play that when a triple five is rolled at any time during a player's turn, their score is reduced to nil and the turn passes to the next player. Call it a tidal wave.

SEQUENCES

This is an easy, fast-moving game, and another one based solely on the luck of the dice, so children and adults are in equally strong positions. It is a good one for children to play to practise their number-sequencing skills.

NUMBER OF PLAYERS	2 to 10
AGE	4 and up
YOU WILL NEED	Six dice, and paper and pencil for scoring
PLAYING TIME	15 to 20 minutes

OBJECT OF THE GAME
To be the first player to score 100 points.

HOW TO PLAY
Decide who will start, and then the first player rolls all six dice and scores for any sequences thrown (see below). If there are no sequences, there is no score, and play passes to the left. Players get just one throw per turn.

Players can score for more than one sequence in a turn; however, any single die can only be attributed to a single sequence. For example, if Tom rolls four, five, one, two, three, four, he scores 20 points: five points for the first sequence and 15 for the second. Apart from sequences, points can also be won by throwing five sixes or six sixes. Any player who throws four ones immediately loses his score for the entire game, and must begin again at zero.

The first player to reach 100 points wins.

Scoring table:

NUMBER OF DICE IN SEQUENCE	SCORE
Two (for example: one, two)	five points
Three (for example: one, two, three)	ten points
Four (for example: one, two, three, four)	15 points
Five (for example: one, two, three, four, five)	20 points
Six (for example: one, two, three, four, five, six)	30 points
Five sixes	40 points
Six sixes	60 points

THIRTY-SIX

Another simple, fun game that helps kids with arithmetic and memory, Thirty-Six is also well suited to some benign gambling.

NUMBER OF PLAYERS	2 to 10
AGE	6 and up
YOU WILL NEED	One die; paper and pencil for scoring (optional); sultanas, nuts, or anything else you choose to bet with (also optional)
PLAYING TIME	10 minutes

OBJECT OF THE GAME
To score 36, or close to it, but no more.

HOW TO PLAY
If you wish to gamble, put a handful of sultanas, say, in a central pot. The first player then rolls the die once, and makes a mental note of its value, before passing it left to the next player, who does the same. Play continues thus around the circle, with each player mentally logging their cumulative score when it is their turn. It's fun to play without writing anything down, so that you use your brains and fingers to add things up and you have to work at remembering your score in between turns. If, however, this proves too much after a long day, just use pen and paper.

When a player's score nears 36, decisions have to be made. If your score exceeds 36, you 'bust' and are out of the game; so, if you get to around 33, you are likely to want to 'stick' and roll no more. How daring are you? It is fun to talk together about probabilities at this point. When each player has either bust or stuck, the person who scores 36, or closest to it, wins the kitty. Yum.

FARKLE

There is some friendly debate in the dice world about where this game started. Some say it began on French sailing ships some 600 years ago (in France, it is called *Dix Mille*, or Ten Thousand), while others argue it was created in Iceland in the 15th century, by a fellow named Sir Albert Farkle (yes, you can't help but smile). Either way, it is a superb game of jeopardy, made even more exciting by being scored in the thousands.

NUMBER OF PLAYERS	2 to 10
AGE	7 and up
YOU WILL NEED	Six dice this time, and paper and pencil for scoring
PLAYING TIME	20 to 30 minutes

OBJECT OF THE GAME
To be the first player to reach 10,000 points.

HOW TO PLAY
The first player rolls all six dice, calculating points according to the various scoring combinations below. If no points are scored, play passes to the left; however, if there is a scoring combination, the player must decide whether to bank the points or to remove a single die and roll again to see whether she can accumulate more points. If, on a second roll with five dice, the player does not score (this is called a Farkle), she loses all her points, and play passes to the left. However, if the player has scored a second time, she is faced with the same decision: bank the score from the first two rolls, or remove yet another die and roll again. The turn continues until the score is banked or the player rolls a Farkle (a non-scoring roll). Each time the dice are rolled again, one more die is left out. Note: in the special case where a player manages to score with all six dice on the first roll, she can roll all six again, if she chooses to gamble.

Scoring combinations are:

Ones	100 points each
Fives	50 points each
Three of a kind	100 x the number (except for ones)
Three ones in a roll	1000 points
A straight of one, two, three, four, five, six in the first roll	1500 points
Note: if three fives are rolled, the score is 500, as with a three of a kind.	

An example of play follows:

Con rolls one, four, three, one, six, one. This roll scores 1000, for three ones. He banks his score and passes the dice to Steven. Steven rolls four, five, two, two, six, two. This scores 250, for three twos plus 50 for one five. He decides to gamble and now rolls just five dice: one, three, five, four, six. This scores another 150 (100 points for the one, and 50 points for the five), so his cumulative score is now four hundred. He gambles again and rolls four dice: four, three, three, two. Oops! No score. It's a Farkle! (Yes, you will enjoy saying this). Play passes to the left and continues around the circle until someone reaches 10,000 points.

VARIATION

You can play with an additional scary penalty, whereby rolling six of anything on that first toss (for example, six twos) results in the player's entire score, from the beginning of the game, being wiped out.

YACHT

This is the game from which the best-selling commercial dice game Yahtzee was born, invented by a Canadian couple on their yacht in 1954. It involves rolling the dice three times on each turn to try to achieve a number of set combinations. A delicious after-dinner-mint of a game.

NUMBER OF PLAYERS	2 to 10
AGE	7 and up
YOU WILL NEED	Five dice, and paper and pencil for drawing up your scoring table
PLAYING TIME	30 minutes

OBJECT OF THE GAME
To be the player with the highest score at the end of the game, when all categories have been filled — that is, after 13 rounds.

HOW TO PLAY
First, you need to make up a score sheet, like the one on the opposite page. We used to do this afresh each time but, recently, we harnessed the power of our computer for good and printed up a wad of tables, which gets us into the game quicker.

For anyone who has played poker, some of these categories are self-explanatory. This is what they are and how they are scored: for the top half of the table, one point is gained for each one thrown; two points for each two thrown, and so on. If a player achieves a score of at least 63 points for the first six categories (the equivalent of having rolled three of each number), he achieves a bonus of 35 points.

In the bottom half, three of a kind is the face value of all dice when at least three of them are the same number. Ditto for four of a kind. Full house is three of one number and two of another, earning a score of 25 points. A short straight is any run of four dice, for example, two, three, four, five; and a long straight is a run of all five dice, either one through to five or two through to six. A short straight earns 30 points, and a long straight 40 points. The Yacht is all five dice of the same number — 50 points. 'Chance' is your one opportunity to score when the dice have given you nothing: it is simply the face value of all dice added up.

	Player 1	Player 2	Player 3	Player 4	Player 5	Player 6
1s						
2s						
3s						
4s						
5s						
6s						
Bonus						
Subtotal						
3 of a kind						
4 of a kind						
Full house						
Short straight						
Long straight						
The Yacht						
Chance						
Subtotal						
TOTAL						

To play, the first player rolls all five dice and, on the basis of what numbers come up, decides which category he will be aiming for — although this can change in the course of a turn. He then has two more rolls to try to complete the category (that is, up to three rolls in one turn), each time putting aside the dice he wishes to keep. If, however, he wishes to score after just one or two rolls, that's fine, too.

By the end of the third throw, the score has to be attributed to one of the categories, even if it is a zero because the dice haven't provided a scoring combination. Afterwards, this score cannot be changed, and no category can be scored twice.

An example of a single turn: Susan rolls two, four, five, five, six. She keeps the two fives, and rolls the other three dice: one, three, five. She keeps this third five, then rolls the remaining two dice, coming up with two and two. She can either score this as 15, under her fives at the top of the table, or score it as a full house, or three of a kind, in the bottom half, depending on which categories she has already filled.

After 13 rounds, the game is over and subtotals from the top and bottom halves of the score sheet are added to make the total. The player with the highest score wins. Often, it's the player who has managed to roll a Yacht.

GAMES OF MARBLES

We would hazard a guess that there are children out there, right now, who have not had the pleasure of shooting marbles. And yet, humans have been playing with marbles for thousands of years. Homemade clay marbles, dried by the sun, were found in Egyptian tombs and Native American burial grounds. (This type of clay homemade jobbie is called a 'marrididdle'.) Later, people began making marbles out of stone, wood, steel, agate, china, and glass. In 1848, a mould was invented that revolutionised marble making, and in 1890 the first machine-made marbles hit the streets of Europe and the United States. Then, in 1950, something else very exciting (for marble lovers) happened: someone in Japan injected coloured glass into a normal marble, and what do you know, a cat's eye was created. Veeery pretty.

Marbles have been around a long time, and their popularity has been enduring; however, with the recent advent of television, computer games, and an endless stream of mass-produced toys, marbles have fallen out of fashion. So, when we introduced our kids to marbles recently, we weren't sure how it would go. It was love at first sight. Now, they go off alone to play with their marbles, practising their techniques and chattering about cat's eyes and taws and spans and snops.

Most marbles games are designed to be played outdoors, but we have included here a handful of games that work well on carpet or a rug. Floorboards are not a good surface for playing marbles. And there is one last important matter to consider before you embark. Historically, children kept their own special collection of marbles in a little drawstring bag or tin and, when they played with one another, they played 'for keeps'; that is, you got to keep what you won at the end of the game. This element of the game went into disfavour for a while (it causes the odd argument). If you choose to play for keeps, it adds excitement to the game and is a lesson in letting things go (and then winning them back later). If you prefer, you can play a 'friendly', where you agree to return marbles to their rightful owners at the end of a game. Or you might just keep a central stash for the whole family to play with. Work this out before you start playing, then take aim and shoot.

SHOOTING TO WIN

There are three common ways to shoot a marble: trolling, hoisting and, the most popular, knuckling down. To 'troll', you simply project the marble along the ground towards its target. 'Hoisting' is when the marble is shot from knee level or above while the player is standing. 'Knuckling down' is by far the most popular, but also the trickiest, method. Players can choose their own technique in any game, although hoisting might be a bit over-zealous for indoor marbles.

TO KNUCKLE DOWN:

1. Curl your fingers up gently, and rest your thumb behind your index finger. Practise flicking it forward (this movement shoots the marble.)
2. Rest the marble in the cranny made by your curled index finger and your thumb. Tighten the index finger, to hold the marble there.
3. And now, 'knuckle down': keeping your hand as still as possible, rest the knuckle of your index fingers on the ground, and flick your thumb to send the marble flying forward to meet its target (we hope).

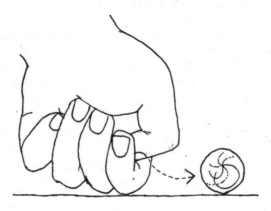

As with everything else in life, the more you knuckle down, the better you get at it. It is a skill that can be honed over many, many games of marbles. Eventually, you should be able to shoot with sufficient force to propel the marble several feet.

WHICH MARBLE WILL I SHOOT WITH?

This is a matter of trial and error, but people who become addicted to marbles can get quite attached to, and possessive of, their chosen one. When you have found your favourite marble for shooting with, it is called your 'taw'. Note that big marbles, 'tomtrollers', are fun to collect, but are not so good for shooting with; ditto the very small marbles, or 'peewees'.

WHO SHOOTS FIRST?

To determine order of play in a game of marbles, set up a marble and a starting line, and all players take a single shot at the target. The player whose marble gets closest starts, second closest goes second, and so on, until the person whose marble is furthest away goes last. A different, and opposite, approach is to allow the youngest, and likely least skilful, player to start first.

SPANS AND SNOPS

This is a simple game, and the one our kids seem to play the most. It is lovely to watch their techniques improve as the weeks go by. The youngest of the kids started with a kind of flicking motion, but has recently joined his older brother in learning to knuckle down.

NUMBER OF PLAYERS	2
AGE	5 and up
YOU WILL NEED	A carpet or rug, and between 5 and 10 marbles each
PLAYING TIME	10 minutes

OBJECT OF THE GAME

To win the most marbles; or, if you want a longer game (or have fewer marbles), to win all the marbles.

HOW TO PLAY

Decide at the start of the game whose hand you're going to use to span the marbles, so as to keep the measurement consistent. Players start with an equal number of marbles and sit themselves on the rug at an agreed distance apart — this can be increased as their game improves. Each player places one marble on the rug in front of them.

The first player starts by shooting at his opponent's marble. If he hits it, this is called a 'snop', and he wins the marble outright. If he gets close, the elder child, or an adult, spans the two relevant marbles with a spread hand, and if they are within the hand-span (you should be able to touch both marbles at the same time) the marble is won: a 'span'. If they are too far apart, however, the first player gets to retrieve his taw, but not the target. In either case, it is the second player's turn to try to win the first player's marble.

Each time a marble is captured, the losing player has to put a new one in front of them, and play continues thus, taking turns, for an agreed number of turns, or until all marbles have been won by one player.

VARIATION

If you only have a couple of marbles, you can play this game with two people, sitting side by side, with one marble placed at a distance from them. Players take turns to shoot at the marble, winning it either through a span or a snop, with scores being tallied. Each time, the marble is replaced in the same location and shot at again with the taw. The player with the greatest number of captures after an agreed number of turns is the winner.

PICKING PLUMS

Another terrific game of marbles that is great for practising technique.

NUMBER OF PLAYERS	2 to 6
AGE	5 and up
YOU WILL NEED	A carpet or rug, and at least 10 marbles to shoot at, plus a taw for each player
PLAYING TIME	5 to 10 minutes

OBJECT OF THE GAME
To pick the most plums (marbles).

HOW TO PLAY
Line up ten or more marbles in an even row, with a minimum of 10cm between each marble. Players crouch at an agreed distance behind a starting line, called an 'offing', and take turns trying to shoot the marbles. If no marble is hit, play moves to the next person; but, if a marble is knocked off, the player collects the marble and tries again. His turn lasts as long as he is successfully 'picking plums', ending when he misses.

Play continues thus, taking turns in an agreed order, until all the plums have been picked. The player with the most plums wins the game.

RING TAW

This is the quintessential game of marbles. Traditionally, this is played outside, with a ring drawn in the dirt, but you can play it inside, using a little imagination. It is helpful (but not necessary) in this game for each player to use a different colour or type of marble to easily distinguish them.

NUMBER OF PLAYERS	2 to 6
AGE	5 and up
YOU WILL NEED	2 marbles per player, and a playing ring of 50 to 80cm in diameter (start off smaller and get bigger as your shooting improves). We draw the ring into the pile of our rug, with a finger; or you can get a length of coloured cotton (string is too thick) and lay it down in a loose circle.
PLAYING TIME	5 to 10 minutes

OBJECT OF THE GAME
To capture the most marbles.

HOW TO PLAY

Each player puts one marble into the ring in a random pattern, and retains a taw for shooting with. Create an offing a short distance away from the ring, depending on skill level.

To begin the game, the youngest player knuckles down at the starting line and shoots, aiming to knock a marble out of the ring. If he is successful, and both the targeted marble and his taw roll outside the ring, he gets to keep the captured marble and take another turn; but, this time, he shoots from the point at which his taw came to rest. However, if he knocks a marble out of the ring and his taw is left inside, he is out of the game and has to put any marbles he has won back into the ring. If he doesn't manage to knock any marbles outside the ring but his taw rolls outside, it stays in this position until it is his turn again, and he shoots from this position. A player also goes out if, at any point, another player hits his taw, in which case he must retire and give up any marbles that he has won to the owner of the striking taw.

Players take turns in an agreed order until there are no marbles in the ring.

ODD OR EVEN

This is the only marbles game we know that involves no trolling, hoisting, or knuckling down, only guesswork. It is a fun, fast game for two, good to fill an idle 15 minutes while dinner is cooking.

NUMBER OF PLAYERS	2
AGE	5 and up
YOU WILL NEED	5 marbles each
PLAYING TIME	5 minutes

OBJECT OF THE GAME

To capture all the marbles.

HOW TO PLAY

The first player puts her marbles and her hands behind her back. She encloses any number of marbles, between one and five, into one hand, before bringing it forward, fist closed. She now asks her opponent to guess whether it holds an odd or an even number. If her opponent guesses correctly, he wins one of her marbles and adds it to his own collection; if he is incorrect, he has to give up one of his own.

It is then the second player's turn to fill his fist with marbles, and the first player has to guess: odd or even? Play continues, taking turns, until one person has won all the marbles.

By the very last go, when all but one marble has been captured, the winning player will be able to deduce the correct answer, so this is a good game for kids learning to count.

MARBLE ARCH

Also known as Bridge-Board, this is great fun, and kids will love making the arches to shoot the marbles through. A mini games arcade in your own parlour!

NUMBER OF PLAYERS	3 to 8
AGES	5 and up
YOU WILL NEED	A strip of cardboard at least 60cm long and 5cm wide (or tape two shorter pieces together), and two small squares of cardboard to make the board stand up; a cup and nail scissors for making the arches; textas for writing numbers on the board; and at least 7 marbles per player
PLAYING TIME	10 mins

OBJECT OF THE GAME
To win the most marbles by the end of the game.

HOW TO PLAY
To make the Marble Arch, use the top of an upside-down cup and a texta to trace six arches, about 3cm high and 5cm wide, into the cardboard strip, with a couple of centimetres between each arch. Cut out the arches, and cut slits into the bottom of either end of the strip. Put small wedges of cardboard

crossways into the slits to make the board stand up. Above each arch, write any number below seven, and in any order. For example: five, two, one, zero, three, four. The lower numbers should be in the middle of the bridge, and the higher ones at the sides.

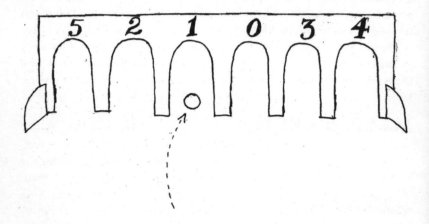

Each player starts with seven or more marbles (can be more, as long as all players have the same number). One player is elected arch-keeper, and the rest retreat behind an offing that faces the board about a metre back, depending on skill level. Decide the order of play, and then the first player shoots, aiming to get her marble through one of the arches. Every marble that fails to go through is won by the arch-keeper; but, for every successful shot, the arch-keeper has to pay out the corresponding number of marbles (written above the arch) to the shooter. Depending on the skill of the players, the arch-keeper often comes off best, so this position can be rotated each round.

The person who has the most marbles after an agreed number of rounds, say, five, is winner.

GAMES OF KNUCKLEBONES

Knucklebones were first used as dice by the Greeks and Romans, thrown to generate random numbers. But the primitive game of Knucklebones, where bones are thrown into the air and caught on the back of the hand, was very much a game of skill and dexterity, rather than luck. Believed to have originated in the Orient many thousands of years ago, and known variously as Jackstones, Jacks, Chuckstones, Fivestones, Hucklebones, Dibs, and Dibstones, the game of Knucklebones has changed little since ancient times. Indeed, a painting excavated at Pompeii shows the goddesses Latona, Niobe, Phoebe, Aglaia, and Hileaera engaged in a hearty game of Knucklebones.

Knucklebones can be played with any five small objects of sufficient weight that they can land on the back of your hand without bouncing off. In Victorian England, owning real knucklebones was an indication of class: it meant your family was able to afford leg of lamb. Poorer children had to play with pebbles or beans or bits of wood. You can purchase Made in China fluorescent-plastic 'knucklebones'; but, in our opinion, a small piece of bright-green plastic shaped like a bone looks ready-made for landfill. As children, we were fortunate enough to learn Knucklebones with a set of five rough old bones at our grandparents' dining-room table, with our grandfather's rough old hands guiding ours. You may have an inherited a set of knucklebones, or someone you know may have an old set tucked away and be thrilled to see them in use. Or you can source and prepare your own (see p. 215).

The game of Knucklebones is fabulous for improving hand–eye coordination. The game can be tailored to suit children of different ages, and you can vary the length by adding or removing throws from the sequence. There are dozens and dozens of variations to this game; we have included here some of the best-known throws. They should keep you going for a good, long time. Meanwhile, ask around and see what other throws you can add to the sequence.

Playing Knucklebones is hard. It requires patience and perseverance and endless practice. It is also addictive. We keep a set of knucklebones on the kitchen counter and, in the course of the day, everyone in the family will take their turn at picking them up and having a play.

NUMBER OF PLAYERS	1 and up
AGES	7 and up
YOU WILL NEED	5 knucklebones, stones, small pieces of tanbark, shells, peach pits, or whatever else you find that works. Smaller hands will benefit from smaller objects. Be inspired.
PLAYING TIME	limitless

OBJECT OF THE GAME

To be the first to successfully complete a series of set throws in an agreed sequence.

HOW TO PLAY

Knucklebones is a game you can play alone. When playing in a group, let the youngest start, before moving clockwise around the circle. You will need a large playing surface: a table or the floor.

Before commencing, players need to agree on the sequence of throws that they will aim to complete. If you are new to Knucklebones, start with 'Ones' through to 'Fours', and start adding new levels as you go. See, it's just like playing a computer game.

Players get one attempt at a throw. If successful, they can progress on the same turn to the next throw. If unsuccessful, the turn moves to the player to their left, and the first player will have to re-attempt the failed throw on their next turn. Each throw has to be successfully completed before a player can proceed through the sequence.

The winner is the first player to successfully complete the agreed series of throws. If you really get into Knucklebones, and you succeed in all the following throws, the next stage of the challenge is to start over, but this time using your left, or non-dominant, hand. Good luck!

THE THROWS

ONES, TWOS, THREES, FOURS — SWEEPS

In most games of Knucklebones, there is a first basic throw: hold all five bones (or other small objects) in your dominant hand, then toss them up in the air — but not too high! While bones are airborne, turn your hand over and try to catch as many of the bones as you can on the back of the same hand (spread flat). The rest of the bones will fall to the floor or table. Leave them there. Now, toss the bones that you have caught up into the air again, flip your hand over, and re-catch as many as you can in your palm. This is your basic first throw.

However many you have managed to hold on to this way — it may be only one or two — put them to one side, retaining one bone that you will use as your 'sky bone', to toss into the air as you pick up the remaining scattered bones. (In Fivestones, this is called your 'sky stone'.) Now, for your Ones, throw up the sky bone and pick up one of the scattered bones, before catching the airborne bone again in the same hand. Put the bone you have retrieved to one side with the others, but use your sky bone to repeat the movement as you pick up each of the scattered bones, one at a time. When you have succeeded in this, you officially have your Ones and it's time to tackle Twos.

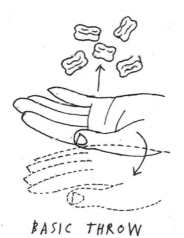

BASIC THROW

For Twos, start with the basic throw, putting to one side any bones you manage to catch and keeping your sky bone. This time, you now have to pick up two bones at a time. If they are scattered far and wide, you can throw the bone up as many times as you need while you sweep them in closer. But if you drop the sky bone at any point while doing this, your turn is over. When they are close enough together, throw sky bone up and pick up two at a time. If there is an odd number, just pick up the one remaining. When you have done this successfully, you have your Twos.

Repeat for Threes and Fours, picking up three and then four bones in a throw. Note: if you are lucky enough to catch two or more bones on the back of your hand in the first step, you still get to put these to one side, so that your Fours may actually entail picking up just one or two scattered bones.

ONES, TWO, THREES, FOURS — SCATTERS

This is the same as Sweeps, but this time you are not allowed to sweep the bones closer together when you are picking them up. So, for Threes, for example, you have to pick up three bones in just one go, however far apart they are. This might look easy, but it can take months of practice.

PECKS

Again, this starts with the basic throw. If you manage to catch all five knucklebones in this first throw, you can cross off Pecks and go straight on to the next challenge. If not, here is what you do: instead of putting any bones you have caught to one side, you keep them all in your clasped hand, but hold your sky bone between your thumb and pointer finger. Toss it into the air while you pick up the scattered bones, one at a time, without dropping any of the bones you are already holding. Repeat until all bones are picked up, but using just one hand.

BUSHELS

Again, if you achieve your basic throw, tick off Bushels, also called Juggles, and move straight to Claws. If not, when you go to retrieve the scattered bones, you have to throw all of the caught bones into the air while you pick up a bone and then re-catch all of the bones in the same hand. Help! Repeat until all bones are picked up.

CLAWS

If you catch all five bones in the basic throw, Claws is done. You should be so lucky. But, if you have caught fewer than five bones on the back of your hand, rather than completing the basic throw, you leave them on the back of your hand while you pick up all the bones from the ground, clasping them between your outstretched fingers, or finger and thumb. Keeping retrieved bones wedged between fingers, toss the bones from the back of the hand up, and catch them in your palm before manoeuvring the retrieved bones into your hand with the rest. If you drop your bundle at this final stage, back to the start of Claws, and try again. Note: the next few games do not start with the basic throw. And remember, if the sky bone is dropped during any of these throws, your turn ends, and you can try again next time.

OVER THE LINE

Lay your non-throwing hand down flat, palm to the ground, and put four bones next to its outer side. Toss up the sky bone and, while airborne, transfer one of the other bones to the other side of your flat hand. Repeat until all four have been moved 'over the line'. Now, toss up the sky bone, and pick all four bones up with your throwing hand before re-catching the sky bone.

OVER THE JUMP

This is the same as Over the Line, but harder, naturally. This time, have your flat non-dominant hand making a vertical wall, with your little finger lying on the ground. Each time the sky bone is airborne, you have to get a bone over the jump, until all bones have reached the other side. On the last throw, pick up all the bones before you catch the sky bone. Voila!

PIGS IN THE PEN: ONES TO FOURS

Scatter bones on the ground. Make an arch, using the thumb and pointer finger of your non-throwing hand. Select a sky bone and throw into the air. While it is airborne, knock the other bones (pigs) through the arch (into the pen), before catching the sky bone. For Ones, push in one pig for each throw. If the sky bone falls to the ground at any point, your turn is over. When all four pigs have been pushed into the pen, the player has to do a final throw, picking up the four bones before catching the sky bone.

This is repeated for Twos, Threes, and Fours; except, in each case, the specified number of bones must be knocked into the pen at the same time.

HORSE IN THE STABLE

Scatter bones again. This time, make a set of stables: arch your non-dominant hand, by having fingertips spread and touching the ground with the rest of hand raised. Select your sky bone, toss it up and, while it is airborne, knock one bone into, or toward, one of the stables. Each bone has to go through a different stable door. Throw, knock, and catch as many times as you need to, until all four stables are filled, then move your non-dominant hand away, toss up the sky bone, and pick up all four bones with your throwing hand before catching the sky bone again.

TOAD IN THE HOLE

Scatter bones. Make a circle (the 'hole') by joining pointer and thumb of your non-throwing hand together. Hold this non-throwing hand parallel to, but just above, the ground, so that bones can fall through it. Throw up the sky bone and, while airborne, pick up one of the other bones (a 'toad'), and drop it into the hole before catching the sky bone. Repeat this until all four toads are in the hole; then, move your non-throwing hand and, while the sky bone is airborne, sweep them all up and catch it again.

THREADING THE NEEDLE

This is the same as Toad in the Hole, but the circle — the eye of the 'needle' — has to be held about 15cm or so above the ground, and the bones are threaded through it.

HOW TO SOURCE AND PREPARE
YOUR OWN KNUCKLEBONES

This is a meaty exercise, so if you are vegetarian, read no further. There are plenty of options for playing knucklebones that use non-animal objects. If, however, you enjoy the odd leg of lamb, and you would like a set of real knucklebones to play with but have not inherited any, here is how you can get your own.

The first step is to find a friendly butcher who is willing to help you out; obviously, you will get nowhere in a supermarket. Local high-street butchers are your best bet, as market butchers tend to be too rushed. At the turn of the last century, city children could still buy knucklebones in sets of five for 'tuppenny' from the local butcher, and their mother would boil them clean,

If you are lucky, your butcher will have played knucklebones as a child and will know exactly which bone you mean. If not, it is called the astragalus or the talus, and it is the only small and complete bone in the knee joint of the lamb. You can find it by cutting into the protective sheathing around the joint: it is roughly rectangular, but has an 's' curve in profile. Remember, it has to be lamb: mutton bones are too big for our purposes. It is a little bit fiddly for your butcher to get the bones out intact but, as an example, over a period of just a few weeks, the butcher we went to had saved us ten knucklebones: two full sets ... or so we thought.

The bones are going to be pretty meaty when you get them, so use a sharp knife to carefully remove excess cartilage or shreds of flesh. This is an adult job. Then, the bones have to be cleaned. First, you need to boil them for half an hour (much longer and they dry out too much and the calcium covering can flake away). Some people add sodium carbonate to the water to help clean off tissue, but it isn't necessary. Some people also add dye to the water, so that they can have coloured bones, while others soak their bones in bleach to make them white. Personally, we like the yellowy look of old bones. After boiling, you can pick off more bits of flesh with your fingernails or a knife.

You might be ready to play now, but if there is anything meaty left on the bones, you can finish cleaning them the natural way, which doubles up as a fun science experiment. Put the bones into a glass jar with large holes in the lid. Put the jar outside in a safe place, where domestic or wild animals won't get it but creepy crawlies can. Leave the jar for several weeks, and allow ants and other carrion-eating insects to clean the bones for you. This is time-consuming but effective, and it is fun to pop outside every few days and see what is going on.

But be warned: if you are going to put your bones outdoors to be cleaned by insects, use glass, not plastic takeaway containers. We tried this, grabbing the first thing that came to hand (ah, the temptations and pitfalls of the modern world), and came home the next afternoon to find the dog had got the container down off a window ledge, broken the plastic open, and chewed up a few bones. Fortunately, there were still enough in good shape to make one full set.

Thank you very much to Macelleria Salumeria Italiana, Australian–Continental Butcher, North Carlton.

WORDS BIG AND SMALL, LONG AND TALL

GAMES SPOKEN ALOUD

According to Australian children's folklorist Dr June Factor, 'poetry is the first language of children — prose, you have to learn. Some poets would give their right arm to have all the techniques that children use in their own chants and song.'

Children play games with language naturally; they love to find the rhythms in it, inverting it and making it do kooky things. Earlier last century, popular Russian children's poet Kornei Chukovsky called it doing 'topsy-turvies' with language. Dr Factor adds that 'verbal play is a great way of mastering the language. It's about the enrichment of language flexibility, about language vocabulary, about language rhythm and metaphor.' The enduring popularity of books by Theodore Seuss Giesel (Dr Seuss) and others, such as Carroll's *Alice's Adventures in Wonderland*, attest to our love affair with language that moves from silly to surreal.

Given children's natural interest in the rhythms of language, it comes as no surprise that spoken games have a long and illustrious history in the parlour. One of the most enduring parlour games, Crambo, is thought to have been played from the 14th century onwards. In the 18th and 19th centuries, no self-respecting gathering of either adults or children would have been complete without a few rounds of Crambo. The spoken games of the late-19th-century parlour were sometimes quite involved, including sophisticated scripts, or extensive knowledge of proverbs, similes, and the like. For a modern audience, we have dispensed with some of the more convoluted games, including instead only those that are very fun to play while still posing some good brain-bending challenges. Many spoken games have proven to be so much fun that they led to popular television shows (such as Twenty Questions and Celebrity Head on *Hey Hey It's Saturday*), radio programs (the BBC's *Just a Minute*), and many a board game (Balderdash, based on the game Dictionary, for example).

One of the best things about spoken games is that they can be played anywhere: in the car, on the couch, or while doing somersaults. They don't require a lot of planning, and can usually be played spontaneously. Most of our favourites have been played in the few minutes before bedtime, while lazing about on the couch, or just before dinner, when the noise level, for some strange reason, gets a bit out of control.

Often, they are very fast games that rely on quick thinking, so they are great for exercising our brains, as well as our mouths. Many can be adapted to suit young kids; in fact, those requiring a lack of inhibition with words are perfectly suited to young kids. And some even lead to a great deal of laughter and loud discussion.

With some of these games, the fun is in exploring the language, playing with silly patterns, making stuff up, and having a pretty hearty laugh. With some younger players, in particular, the rules can be adapted so that there is less of a focus on competition and more of a focus on fun.

And so, we are proud to present the following games, which focus on guessing, on grabbing letters from behind, and on gibber-gabbing until the geese come home.

What are you waiting for? Put the kettle on, grab a comfortable armchair, and verbalise those voracious vocal skills.

FIRST THINGS FIRST: THE PERFECT POT OF TEA

The history of tea dates back some 4000 years. Legend has it that it was discovered by China's Emperor Shen Nun, when a breeze blew the leaves from a nearby wild tea tree into a pot of boiling water. On tasting the brew, the Emperor was reputedly delighted with its invigorating qualities.

In a bid to do this old and revered beverage justice, we spent a few hours at the State Library of Victoria in search of the definitive recipe for making the perfect brew.

Some 1314 entries came up when we searched under the subject of tea, including material on its origins, its history, and a great many intriguing photographs of it being drunk by corseted ladies and lank soldiers in times gone by. Somewhere amid all this, we were determined to find out how to make the perfect pot.

We started by exploring the illustrated *Tea and Tea Drinking* by Arthur Reade, published in 1884. It arrived from the bowels of the library shrink-wrapped to protect its musty pages — nothing that you download from the internet smells quite like an old book. It chronicled fascinating tales on tea and its travels, but nothing on how to make the perfect brew.

Next, we went in search of a book called *Consumer Culture in the Long Nineteenth Century* by T. S. Wagner. It listed multiple entries on 'tea' in the index, but was more academic than aromatic. No messages there about how to make the perfect pot. Back on the shelf it went.

While looking for that book, we came across a whole section on etiquette. Here, we found bulging tomes on hosting the perfect wedding, slim volumes on getting by at Bar Mitzvahs, and the more generic *Etiquette for Dummies*. We were taken by the sound of *Miss Manners' Guide to Excruciatingly Correct Behaviour* by Judith Martin. Her sardonic pages on 'Afternoon Tea and High Tea' are well worth making a visit to the library for.

In the end, our journey led us to the ever-sensible *Beeton's Book of Household Management* by Isabella Mary Mayson, published in 1861. Thankfully, one of its 2751 entries is on how to make tea. It goes without saying that you will need real leaf tea for this one; tea bags certainly hadn't been invented in Mrs Beeton's day.

MRS BEETON TIP 1814: TO MAKE TEA

There is very little art in making good tea; if the water is boiling, and there is no sparing of the fragrant leaf, the beverage will almost invariably be good. The old-fashioned plan of allowing a teaspoonful to each person, and one over, is still practised. Warm the teapot with boiling water; let it remain for two or three minutes for the vessel to become thoroughly hot, then pour it away. Put in the tea, pour in from ½ to ¾ pint (1 to 1.5 cups) of boiling water, close the lid, and let it stand for the tea to draw from 5 to 10 minutes; then fill up the pot with water. The tea will be quite spoiled unless made with water that is actually 'boiling', as the leaves will not open, and the flavour not be extracted from them; the beverage will consequently be colourless and tasteless, — in fact, nothing but tepid water.

Where there is a very large party to make tea for, it is a good plan to have two teapots instead of putting a large quantity of tea into one pot; the tea, besides, will go farther. When the infusion has been once completed, the addition of fresh tea adds very little to the strength; so, when more is required, have the pot emptied of the old leaves, scalded, and fresh tea made in the usual manner.

GAMES WITH GUESSES

Have you ever noticed the look of delight on a young child's face when there is a guess to be had? Their eyes light up, their interest is piqued and, suddenly, they are yours for the duration of the game. There's the challenge of working out what someone is thinking, of guessing their 'secret', and it is usually by asking questions that we can decipher their thoughts.

Of course, guessing has been around for a long time: the word 'guess' has Scandinavian origins, dating back to the 14th century. It was around this time that one of the early guessing games, ABC of Aristotle, later known as Crambo, was played. In guessing games, the goal is to guess some kind of information, such as a word, a phrase, a title, or the location of an object.

The guessing games on the following pages move from those for especially young players with keen observational skills (as in I Spy and the gimmicky Thought Reading), to perennial favourites such as Twenty Questions, where sound deductive questioning is required. We then take it up a few notches for older players who are very skilled guessers, with clever word games such as Teakettle and the very entertaining Celebrity Heads.

What really matters is what you do with what you have.
— H. G. Wells

I SPY

This is a classic game that's great in the few ratty minutes before dinner, when your hands aren't free but your mouth is; when a child is sick in bed; or when your children are simply waiting for something (anything) to happen. It's also great for young kids who are learning the alphabet.

NUMBER OF PLAYERS	2 or more
AGE	3 and up
YOU WILL NEED	Good observational skills
PLAYING TIME	5 minutes per round

OBJECT OF THE GAME

For players to guess which object a player is thinking of, by observing the objects around them.

HOW TO PLAY

Choose someone to begin the game. The starting player secretly selects an object that everyone can see before saying: 'I spy with my little eye, something beginning with …', naming the letter that the object begins with. The other players then look around for any possible objects beginning with that letter, and take turns to guess what it is.

The first person to successfully guess the object gets to choose the next thing to spy.

VARIATION

When our children were very young, and before they could spell, we played it using colours: for example, 'I spy with my little eye, I see something *green*.'

I SPY WITH MY LITTLE EYE,
I SEE SOMETHING 'GREEN'.

WHAT ANIMAL AM I?

This game is a charming children's version of Celebrity Heads (see p. 230), and is perfect for children's parties. The quiet part of this game is the drawing of the pictures. But once you have pinned them on players' backs, let the noise and laughter begin.

NUMBER OF PLAYERS	3 or more
AGE	4 and up
YOU WILL NEED	Pen and paper, and something to secure the paper to each player's back, such as clothes pegs
PLAYING TIME	10 to 15 minutes per round

OBJECT OF THE GAME

To be the first to guess which animal picture is stuck to your back.

HOW TO PLAY

Each player draws a picture of an animal, taking care that no one sees it. These are stuck on the back of each of the other players (making sure each person does not see the picture on their own back). Players then proceed to ask questions about the animal on their back, such as: 'Is it a sea animal?' 'Is it furry?' 'Is it large?' They are only allowed to ask questions that require 'yes' or 'no' answers. The first person to correctly call out the name of the animal on their back is the winner. The game can continue until all players have guessed their animal (younger children might need some helpful clues if the game goes on too long). Another animal can then be drawn, to settle everyone down, and the game can begin again.

If there is only a small group, players can take it in turns around a circle to ask their questions; at a party, or in a larger group, players can mill about and ask questions of whomever they choose. A small prize may be awarded to the winner.

THOUGHT READING

*In all sleight of hand illusions, the great secret is this:
the hand of the exhibitor must be quicker than the eyes of the audience.*
— C. Gilbert, *Endless Mirth and Amusement*, 1874

Magic and trickery was a popular pastime in the late 19th century, with whole sections of parlour-games books, and indeed whole books, dedicated to its practice. This is a game that will keep the littlies going for a while and give players a good laugh until everyone is in on the trick. While it probably falls between the cracks of a 'spoken' game and that of parlour trickery, we couldn't resist including it here, because half the fun is in guessing what the trick is.

NUMBER OF PLAYERS	3 or more
AGES	4 and up
YOU WILL NEED	To work out the best way of 'communicating' the trick; the ability to keep a straight face
PLAYING TIME	5 to 10 minutes per trick

OBJECT OF THE GAME

For the medium and the thought-reader to execute the trick successfully; and, paradoxically, for the players to work out how they are being stooged.

HOW TO PLAY

The players form a circle. A 'medium' is decided upon, as well as a 'thought-reader'. Both of these players need to be in on the trick. The thought-reader goes out of the room. The group agrees on a number up to ten. When the thought-reader comes back, the medium holds the hand of the thought-reader so as to 'transfer' the thought. While distracting the audience with exaggerated facial expressions, she conveys the number through a series of squeezes. For example, if the secret number is 'four', four soft squeezes are made. The thought-reader then announces the answer confidently. The trick can be repeated as many times as one likes, perhaps with variations (four winks, four raised eyebrows, so long as these have been agreed on beforehand), so that the audience doesn't cotton on.

As with many a good trick, the success of this relies on a bit of bluff and excellent sleight of hand. It might be worth practising with an accomplice before taking it to a wider audience.

TWENTY QUESTIONS

This is the classic parlour game that became the popular American radio quiz show *Twenty Questions* in the 1940s, and that first appeared as a television program in the US in 1949.

It helps kids to concentrate, and it's great for younger players who love having a secret. As players get better and better, their questions become more targeted and the 'secrets' more obscure, which makes it more challenging for distracted parents who might want a fast solution.

NUMBER OF PLAYERS	3 to 13
AGES	5 and up
YOU WILL NEED	The ability to ask sensible questions, and a fine-tuned capacity for deduction
PLAYING TIME	10 to 15 minutes

OBJECT OF THE GAME
To guess the name of the object that is in the mind of the keeper of the 'secret'.

HOW TO PLAY

One person is selected to be the secret-keeper. She thinks of something (anything) which she does not share with the rest of the group. The rest of the players are allowed to ask 20 questions that require 'yes' or 'no' answers. For example, questions might include: 'Is it inside this room?' 'Is it larger than a television?' 'Is it made of plastic?'

If someone thinks they know what it is, they can hazard a guess. If the guess is incorrect, that person is out of that round of the game. If their answer is correct, that person chooses the next word and another round begins. If no one guesses the word once 20 questions have been asked, the same player can choose another word.

DID YOU KNOW?

Simon bar Kokhba, a Jewish leader who reigned around the time of Hadrian (of Hadrian's Wall fame), was reputedly presented with a man who had had his tongue ripped out and his hands cut off. The victim, not able to talk or write, was incapable of saying who his attackers were. Bar Kokhba asked simple questions of the dying man, to which the victim nodded or shook his head. According to legend, the murderers were consequently apprehended.

For this reason, in Hungary, a game not unlike Twenty Questions is named after bar Kokhba. In Hungarian, the common verb *kibarkochbázni* ('to bar Kochba out') means 'retrieving information in an extremely tedious way'.

VARIATION

It is thought that the idea for this game — known as Animal, Vegetable, Mineral — stems from the possibly Renaissance notion that all life was animal or plant (vegetable), and that non-living matter was mineral.

In this version, the questioner thinks of a category and tells the others whether it is animal, vegetable, mineral, or a mixture of these. You can stump players by categorising shoes as 'animal', because they are made of leather; or a doorframe as 'vegetable', because it is made of wood.

The categories are as follows:

Animal	Any animal, including animal products, such as wool or lard. Of course, it includes people.
Vegetable	Anything that is derived from plants that is not an animal. This even includes things like sweet chilli sauce and Vegemite.
Mineral	Any non-living object, like a CD player, a table, or a window.
Mixture	This is where the object includes more than one of the above, but it is usual to say what the main category is.

Once the category has been established, play continues as for Twenty Questions.

Yet another variation, popular with children, is played with the categories Animal, Vegetable, Mineral, Candy. Yum yum, we'll be up for that.

WHO'S CLOSEST

NUMBER OF PLAYERS	3 to 13
AGE	6 and up
YOU WILL NEED	Your sense of humour
PLAYING TIME	5 minutes per round

OBJECT OF THE GAME
To think of the funniest thought you can.

HOW TO PLAY
This game starts with one player thinking any thought at all, for example, 'My mum's got a big bum'. Players then take turns trying to guess what the speaker is thinking.

Once everyone has had their turn, the thinker reveals the actual thought. Everyone then takes it in turns to say why their guess was closest, and the idea is to come up with the most hilarious justification for this. Unless a particular guess was very good, the decision is based mainly on the funniest response. The thinker decides who was closest, and that person becomes the next thinker.

As with many spoken games, this can get quite ridiculous and raucous: definitely not a settling-down-before-bedtime game.

CELEBRITY HEADS

This game is also known as Forehead Detective, The Post-it Game, or The Rizla Game. It made an appearance in an episode of the US series *Six Feet Under*. It's a great icebreaker at a party, or equally fun after dinner.

NUMBER OF PLAYERS	2 to 13
AGE	6 and up
YOU WILL NEED	Paper, pen, and tape, and a fine-tuned capacity for deduction
PLAYING TIME	5 to 10 minutes per round

OBJECT OF THE GAME

To guess the name of the celebrity or famous person on the piece of paper stuck to your forehead.

HOW TO PLAY

The names of famous people or celebrities are written on a bit of paper (sticky notes work well, or a 'dunces' hat, if you have the time to make it beforehand) and stuck, with tape, to the forehead or hat of the player. Care must be taken that the player does not see what is written on their paper.

If there are two players, they can stick the note on each other's heads. If there is a party of players, two or three players can step up and agree to be the 'panel' of celebrities, with all others in the party responding to their questions.

Each player then has to ask questions that allow for a 'yes' or 'no' response to try to decipher who they are. For example, 'Am I human?' 'Am I male?'

'Do I have blond hair?'

Supposing you are playing with a panel, each time a player gets a correct response, they have a chance to ask another question. If the response to their question is 'no', then play continues to the next player. Players can call out their guesses if they think they know who they are; if they are wrong, play passes down the line.

Characters need not only be people: Kermit the Frog, Bugs Bunny, and Humphrey B. Bear might stump players.

The first person to guess their identity wins, and play continues until all players have guessed who they are.

VARIATIONS

The names of celebrities can be written on paper, which is stuck to the backs of guests as they arrive at a party or a games night. Celebrities can be 'coupled' (for example, Mickey and Minnie Mouse) so that once people work out who they are, they also have to find their partner. This is a great icebreaker, particularly at a party of strangers.

If it is a themed party (1920s, for example) you could have gangsters, famous screen stars, and politicians from the era. The first person to correctly guess their identity may win a small prize.

Another variation of this game is Who Am I?, where one player assumes the identity of a famous person, living or dead, and players have to guess the identity of that person by asking questions that require a 'yes' or 'no' response. The person who correctly guesses the answer becomes the next famous person.

COFFEE POT

In this game, the aim is not to guess the identity of a person but rather a verb. The catch is that this verb is replaced by the word 'coffee pot'. This game is great for practising and reviewing action verbs and adverbs, and is thus often used in the teaching of English as a second language. We have to confess that we like it because it's silly.

NUMBER OF PLAYERS	2 to 8
AGE	6 and up
YOU WILL NEED	Good guessing powers
PLAYING TIME	5 minutes per round

OBJECT OF THE GAME
To guess the word that a player is thinking of.

HOW TO PLAY
One player leaves the room, and the other players think of a verb; for example, 'walk'. They must now to replace this word with the word 'coffee pot' at all times. They call the player back in, and she has to ask questions of all the other players in turn to try to guess the word. For example:

Stephanie: 'Do you need any equipment to coffee pot?'
Chrysoula: 'I use my legs when coffee potting.'
Stephanie: 'Is coffee potting good for you?'
Adrian: 'Coffee potting is great for you. It makes you feel really good.'
Stephanie: 'How often do you coffee pot?'
Chrysoula: 'I coffee pot all the time.'

If the player guesses the word, the person that answered the last question leaves the room, and another verb is decided on.

VARIATION
This variation is also used in an educational setting, and is better suited for more experienced players, as it is more abstract. One player chooses a word,

usually an abstract noun, and provides clues to the other players to help them guess what this is.

For example, if the word were 'leader': 'I am a noun ... People often look to me for guidance ... I am guided by laws ... I begin with the letter l.'

The person who guesses correctly chooses the next word.

TEAKETTLE

This game is in a similar vein to Coffee Pot, but is better suited to older players, as it uses homophones, which are words that sound the same but have different meanings. Its roots are in the traditional parlour game How, Why, When, Where, in which the aim was to guess what homophone one player was thinking of by asking only these four questions: 'How do you like it?' 'Why do you like it?' 'When do you like it?' and 'Where do you like it?'

Try this modern version and see if you can guess what the teakettle is.

NUMBER OF PLAYERS	2 or more
AGE	8 and up
YOU WILL NEED	A keen capacity with words
PLAYING TIME	5 to 10 minutes per round

OBJECT OF THE GAME
To guess the pair of homophones that a player is thinking of.

HOW TO PLAY
One player leaves the room, and the other players think of a pair of homophones: for example, 'bare' and 'bear'. When the guesser comes back in, the other players must now replace these words with the word 'teakettle' in a conversation. This might flow as follows:

Adrian: 'I saw a teakettle on television the other day.'
Stephanie: 'Yes, I saw that teakettle, too.'
Chrysoula: 'Teakettles can be so fierce, especially when they teakettle their teeth.'
Adrian: 'But teakettles are really cute when they're asleep.'

Stephanie: 'They are at risk of extinction, as their environment is getting so teakettle.'

It is the job of the guesser to listen carefully and try to guess what the homophones are. Once they have guessed correctly, the player who was speaking last leaves the room for the next round.

CRAMBO

The old game of Crambo, also known as Capping the Rhyme, has had many an illustrious follower, including 17th-century Scottish poet and lyricist Robert Burns; author from the same century James Boswell; and the man credited with founding communism, Karl Marx. Why not add your name to this famous line-up and keep the tradition alive?

NUMBER OF PLAYERS	4 to 12
AGE	8 and up
YOU WILL NEED	Good guessing powers
PLAYING TIME	3 to 5 minutes per word

OBJECT OF THE GAME
To guess the word that a player is thinking of.

HOW TO PLAY
One player thinks of a word and tells the others what it rhymes with. For example, if they are thinking of 'book', they may give the word 'shook'. The other players in the group then have to guess what the word is by asking questions. For example:

Suzy: 'I know a word that rhymes with "shook".'
Mary: 'Is it something you do with your eyes?'
Suzy: 'No, it is not "look".'
Harry: 'Is it something you hang clothes on?'
Suzy: 'No, it is not "hook".'

John: 'Is it something that you read?'
Suzy: 'Yes, it is a book.'

When someone guesses the word, play passes over to the guesser, who then thinks of a new word. If players can't guess the word, the player who thought of the word has another turn.

I KNOW A WORD THAT RHYMES
WITH SNAKE

VARIATION

Dumb Crambo is a similar game but, instead of using words, actions are used to guess the rhyme. This is more suitable for younger kids, and it leads to a fair bit of slapstick hilarity as players try to illustrate words such as 'trip', 'skip', and 'zip'.

Players divide into teams. Half the players leave the room, and the other half decide on a word, which must be a verb. When the other players return, they are given another verb that rhymes with the chosen word. For example, if the verb is 'jump', they may say the word 'lump'.

The team then leaves the room again. They choose three words that rhyme with 'lump' and work out a way to act these out. They come back into the room and mime these, one by one. If they are wrong, the opposing team hiss, boo, and stamp loudly. If they are right, they are applauded and congratulated, and play swaps over.

A quiet game just before bedtime? I think not.

DID YOU KNOW?

According to the *Macquarie Dictionary*, the word 'crambo' is a game in which one person, or side, must find a rhyme to a word or line of verse given by another. The alternative (derogatory) meaning comes from the Latin *'crambe'* meaning cabbage, which is short for *'crambe repetita'* or 'repeated cabbage', and is thought to refer to the repeated rhyming word. Best not to go there.

GAMES WITH LETTERS AND WORDS

Have you ever watched children learning to read sounding out careful word by careful word? Or sat with them as they formed their first letters, gripping their pencils tightly, their faces full of concentration?

Once they have mastered reading and writing, what a wonderful new world opens up: the words on a page suddenly materialise into stories, adventures, and fantastical journeys that take them places. And the more words acquired, the richer and more complex these worlds become.

This section starts with some basic letter and word games for very young kids and progresses to harder ones for cluey wordsmiths, requiring quite sophisticated linguistic skills. Whether younger kids are remembering what they bought at market using their ABCs (I Went to Market), or older children are using the initials of their own name to answer silly questions (Initial Letters), they're sure to have fun and improve their word skills with these games.

I WENT TO MARKET

NUMBER OF PLAYERS	2 to 12
AGE	4 and up
YOU WILL NEED	The ability to remember lots of things
PLAYING TIME	10 to 15 minutes

OBJECT OF THE GAME
To remember an ever-growing list of things.

HOW TO PLAY
Players sit across from each other or, in the case of bigger groups, in a circle. The first player starts off by saying one thing that that they bought from market starting with the letter a. The next player says one thing they bought starting with the letter b, and so on, right through the alphabet. For example:

John: 'I went to market and bought an apple.'

Jenny: 'I went to market and I bought an apple and a broad bean.'

Wei Ling: 'I went to market and I bought an apple, and a broad bean, and a carrot …'

Play continues in this way until one player forgets one of the things that was bought at the market or gets it in the wrong order. They sit out and the game continues. The last person remaining is the winner.

VARIATION

You can also play this game without using the letters of the alphabet, making it even harder to remember what was bought.

EARTH, AIR, WATER, FIRE

Also known as The Elements, this is a dear game that has been requested time and time again in our houses. Because it involves throwing a hanky (sometimes quite vigorously), there is an extra element of fun to the wordplay.

NUMBER OF PLAYERS	3 or more
AGE	5 and up
YOU WILL NEED	A hanky (or a few scrunched-up tissues, if you can't find such an old-fashioned accoutrement)
PLAYING TIME	5 minutes per round

OBJECT OF THE GAME
To think quickly of an animal within each of the nominated categories.

HOW TO PLAY
Players sit in a circle. One player throws a screwed-up handkerchief to another player, stating either 'earth', 'fire', 'water', or 'air', and then counting energetically up to ten. The person who catches the handkerchief has to come up with an animal that lives on the ground (earth), a bird or an insect (air), or an animal that lives in the water (water). If 'fire' is called out, however, the person who catches the handkerchief has to throw it to someone else, quickly, as if it is on fire. If a player cannot think of a word before the counting has finished, they are out of that round. The last person to remain in the round is the winner.

THE LIGHTNING GAME

This game gets its name from the fact that players have to be as fast as lightning to think of as many words as they can that start with a particular letter. It sounds easy, but many of us have got stuck under pressure. It's a game that is great for young kids as well as older ones. If you have a mixed group, it's best if people focus on their 'personal best' score, as six-year-olds trying to compete with 14-year-olds will no doubt lead to tears.

NUMBER OF PLAYERS	2 or more
AGE	5 and up
YOU WILL NEED	Pen and paper to keep score, and a watch with a second hand
PLAYING TIME	5 to 10 minutes per round

OBJECT OF THE GAME
To think of as many words as you can that start with a nominated letter of the alphabet.

HOW TO PLAY
One player chooses a letter. Each player then takes it in turns to call out as many words as they can in one minute, all starting with the chosen letter. Someone keeps time and score, and play moves around the group to see how many words can be thought of with that letter within the minute. In the next round, another player chooses a different letter, and play continues around the group. Words can be repeated but are only scored the first time.

The scores are added up at the end, and the player with the highest score is the winner. If the abilities or ages of the group are mixed, players can focus on their own personal scores and see if they improved as the game progressed.

A SIMPLE ALPHABET GAME

This alphabet game is one that leads to a fair bit of ridiculous wordplay — especially for younger players, who are prone to making words up to get them to fit the rules.

NUMBER OF PLAYERS	2 or more
AGE	6 and up
YOU WILL NEED	Knowledge of the alphabet
PLAYING TIME	10 to 15 minutes

OBJECT OF THE GAME

To think of a four-word sentence in which each word starts with the same letter, as quickly as you can.

HOW TO PLAY

The first player must come up with four words beginning with the letter a. Play continues around the group with each subsequent letter of the alphabet.

For example:

Mary: 'Anna asked Annie again.'
Jane: 'Bold Billy Bob bowed.'
Chrysoula: 'Candy cooks Chinese cabbage.'
Mary: 'Daggy Dick does doodledoos.'

If a player gets stuck and can't make up a word by the time the others have counted to ten, they are out. For younger players, you may dispense with the counting and let them take their time. Play continues around until there is only one player left.

It is best to agree at the outset if made-up words will be allowed (highly desirable and often very amusing in the case of younger players), or if this will be a serious game of wordsmithery.

CANDY COOKS
CHINESE CABBAGE.

ASSOCIATIONS

This game must be played quickly, without hesitation, otherwise it loses its point. Because it's quick and dirty, it can lead to lots of hilarity and raised voices, as people come out with strange (and sometimes embarrassing) associations that they must explain.

NUMBER OF PLAYERS	2 to 12
AGE	6 and up
YOU WILL NEED	An ability to think quickly and on your feet (even if you are sitting down)
PLAYING TIME	10 minutes per game

OBJECT OF THE GAME
To create a long chain of correctly associated words, demonstrating the ability to explain yourself creatively if the associations are a little far-fetched.

HOW TO PLAY
The first player says a word, any word. The second player calls out an associated word, and so on. For example:

Jane: 'Cow'
Jack: 'Milk'
Jill: 'Drink'
Jane: 'Run'

In this example, how is the word 'drink' connected to 'run'? Jane might say that every time she has a drink, she needs to run to the toilet. In this way, anyone can be challenged on an association and asked to explain themselves.

If everyone deems it an allowable association, the person who made the challenge is out. In the case of a smaller group, the person loses one of three chances (or 'lives'), in the interests of continuity. If the association is not acceptable to the players, the person who made the ill-fated association is out. Those that cannot think of an association or hesitate too long are also out.

The game continues until only one player is left, and this person is declared the winner.

THE MINISTER'S CAT

This game also works through letters of the alphabet. This time, players need to think of adjectives to describe the minister's cat. A fun and frivolous way to while away a few stray minutes.

NUMBER OF PLAYERS	2 to 8
AGES	6 and up
YOU WILL NEED	Lots of creative ways to describe the minister's cat
PLAYING TIME	10 minutes

OBJECT OF THE GAME
To work through the alphabet to describe the minister's cat.

HOW TO PLAY
Each player describes the minister's cat using an adjective starting with the first letter of, and then moving through, the alphabet. For example:

Mary: 'The minister's cat is an admirable cat.'
John: 'The minister's cat is an angry cat.'
Sarah: 'The minister's cat is an anti-social cat.'
Mary: 'The minister's cat is a beautiful cat.'
John: 'The minister's cat is a brave cat.'
Sarah: 'The minister's cat is a brazen cat.'

In this way, players see how many creative adjectives they can find to describe the minister's cat. Those that can't think of a word, or repeat a word that has already been said, drop out. Younger players might need some prompting to help them keep up.

VARIATION
A similar game to The Minister's Cat, but for slightly older players, is I Love My Love. Instead of describing the minister's cat, players must work their way through the alphabet to describe why they love their love. In the parlour version of this game, players had to work through a fairly rigid structure but,

for our modern audience, we have kept it more low-key: players can say they love their love, what his or her name is, how they are together, and what they cook for their love, as per the following example:

Fatima: 'I love my love because he is angelically agile and appropriate, and his name is Arthur. We are amorous, and I cook him aubergines.'
Jenny: 'I love my love because he is beautifully bulky and bombastic, and I always call him Bubsy. We are bubbly, and I cook him baba ganoush.'
Max: 'I love my love because she is cat-like, cute, and cuddly, and her pet name is Coochy-Coo. We are carefree and I cook her carrots.'

The game can be played with winners and losers, as for The Minister's Cat, or simply for the sheer joy of seeing how clever and silly players can get.

GRAB ON BEHIND

This game is a fun way to test (or build) your knowledge about a particular topic; for example, cars, dog breeds, or musical artists.

NUMBER OF PLAYERS	2 or more
AGE	7 and up
YOU WILL NEED	Knowledge about your chosen topic; a watch or clock with a second hand
PLAYING TIME	3 to 5 minutes per round

OBJECT OF THE GAME

To be the quickest to think of a word within a chosen category that begins with the last letter of the preceding player's word.

HOW TO PLAY

First, players decide on a category, such as plants, countries, car makes, dog breeds, birds, or mammals. For younger kids (and challenged or sleep-deprived parents), more general categories like animals or things around the house can be used. For older kids, it might be bands or movies. To add an educational component, you may like to choose topics that kids are learning about at school.

The first player calls out a word in the chosen category. The next player follows with another word in the same category, but it must start with the last letter of the first player's word. A little bit of mental gymnastics is required here. For example, if the category is animals, then someone might call out 'monkey'. What animal starts with y? 'Yak,' pipes up a clever player.

Play continues around the group in this way. Players count to ten slowly as the person is thinking of their word. They are not allowed to repeat any word that has already been used.

Anyone who fails to think of a word quickly enough, or who calls out an incorrect word, is out. The last player to stay in wins, and a new topic can be decided on.

SPELLING BEES

'My spelling is Wobbly. It's good spelling but it Wobbles,
and the letters get in the wrong places.'
— Winnie the Pooh

Games that test spelling were very popular in the parlour, and their appeal still endures in the classroom as a teaching tool. In the United States, spelling-bee competitions abound. If the 2004 documentary *Spellbound* is anything to go by, the level of competition in a United States National Spelling Bee is up there with any Olympic sport. Our suggestion? Don't forget to have fun.

NUMBER OF PLAYERS	3 to 12
AGE	8 and up
YOU WILL NEED	A dictionary, pen and paper, and a container
PLAYING TIME	10 to 15 minutes per round

OBJECT OF THE GAME
To spell the most number of words correctly.

HOW TO PLAY
If playing with younger children, an adult can select age-appropriate words. Older children can choose around ten words each from the dictionary, write these down, and place them in a container.

Players form a line. Someone is chosen as the designated 'teacher', and they stand at the top of a line. The second person down the line is asked to spell a word, taken from the container. If they spell it correctly, they are 'safe' and go to the back of the line, and a new word is provided to the next player. If they are wrong, they step out of that round and become a spectator. Play moves down the line, and the next player must guess how to spell the same word that the previous player got wrong. Play continues until, gradually, only two players are left. A great deal of encouragement and cheering is showered on these two players, and the sense of competition heightens. They are given more words to spell until someone gets it wrong. The last person standing is declared the winner.

This game is best played in a bigger group, among children with similar abilities. Play can rotate, so that everyone gets a chance to be the designated 'teacher'. Unusual or funny words can be used to challenge and amuse players and spectators alike. If everyone is spelling the words correctly and no one is dropping out, harder words may need to be selected. Similarly, if everyone is struggling with the chosen words, easier ones may need to be chosen. Helpful adults may need to come in at this point, if they are not already involved.

VARIATION
Add a layer of difficulty by having players spell words backwards.

INITIAL LETTERS

This is a novel game that requires players to respond to questions with answers that start with the initials of their name. It sounds easy, but if there are three people in your group who all have the initial 'm' (or, even worse, if someone has two 'm's in their name, like our friend Monica Marshall), or if your surname starts with 'x', then you will be seriously challenged.

NUMBER OF PLAYERS	2 to 12
AGE	9 and up
YOU WILL NEED	The ability to think quickly and creatively
PLAYING TIME	10 to 15 minutes

OBJECT OF THE GAME
To be the quickest to think of an accurate response to any question using two words that each start with one of the two initials of your name.

HOW TO PLAY
Players sit across from each other (if there are only two), or in a circle (if there are more). One player puts either a serious or silly question to the other players. Each player in turn must answer with a two-word reply, with each

word beginning with the initials of their own name.

So, for instance, if the question is: 'What colour are Grandma's undies?' Mary Jones might say, 'Mauve and jade.' The second player, John Brown, might say, 'Just blue.' Is 'just blue' a colour? It would be up to the group to say if this was allowed.

Any player who cannot answer, or who gives a wrong or inadmissible answer, drops out of the round. When the remaining players have answered the first question, play continues around the group with another question. The winner is the last person standing.

If you get really good at this, you can add an extra layer of difficulty by timing people (five seconds for older players, 20 seconds for younger players, for example).

VARIATION

Decide on a category, such as fruit. Play goes around in a circle, with all players stating what fruit they are. The fruit they choose must start with the initial of their first name. They then also have to state what was said before them.

For example:

Sophia: 'Sophia the strawberry.'
Belinda: 'Sophia the strawberry, Belinda the blackberry.'
Rebecca: 'Sophia the strawberry, Belinda the blackberry, Rebecca the raspberry.'

Play continues in this way until players step out, either because they forget the names or fruits of those who went before them or because they can no longer think of a new fruit starting with the initial of their name. The last person remaining wins.

GHOSTS

Also known as Never-Ending Words and the Spelling Game, this game is for sophisticated wordsmiths, as it requires players to make about-face turns so as not to be the last to finish a word. OK, a bit of bluff doesn't hurt, either.

NUMBER OF PLAYERS	2 to 6
AGE	10 and up
YOU WILL NEED	A good vocabulary, the ability to bluff, and a dictionary to settle disputes
PLAYING TIME	15 to 20 minutes

OBJECT OF THE GAME
To avoid being the first to complete the spelling of a word.

HOW TO PLAY
Players keep adding letters to make a word, all the while aiming not to be the last to complete the word. At any given time, they must have a real word in mind, but this word usually changes as each person adds their letter. Words of up to three letters don't count, in the interests of keeping the game going. For example:

Nick: 'S.' (He is thinking of the word 'something'.)
Mary: 'SE.' (She is thinking of the word 'see-saw'.)
Nick: 'SEN.' (He is now thinking now of the word 'sentence'.)
Mary: 'SENS.' (She is thinking of 'sensitive'.)
Nick: 'SENSI.' (He has now changed his to 'sensible'.)
Mary: 'SENSIT.' (She adds to the word 'sensitive'.)
Nick: 'SENSITI.' (He adds to the word 'sensitive'.)
Mary: 'SENSITIV.' ('I've got him!' she thinks.)
Nick: 'SENSITIVE.'

Nick, having finished a complete word, loses a life. Players are not allowed to add 'ly' or 'ness', for example, to extend already complete words.

If someone is at a loss, they can bluff, by adding a letter when they have no word in mind. But beware: players can be challenged if someone thinks they are not working towards a bona fide word.

There are three ways in which players can lose a life: if they are 'fibbing' and are challenged correctly, if they mistakenly challenge someone who they think is not working towards a real word, or if they finish a complete word. To challenge someone, players call out 'ghost'.

Players have five lives. If one life is lost, the player gets a 'g'; the loser of two lives gets a 'gh', and so on. The first person to lose five lives is a 'ghost', and has thereby lost the game.

After one player has lost all five lives, the person with the most lives remaining is the winner.

This game is best played with those of a similar level of vocabulary.

CARNELLI

This game works on the same premise as Associations but, instead of words, players think of associated titles, such as those of a book, play, movie, or song. This game has a cult following at Mensa (the high-IQ society) meetings in the US, and was created by Jan Carnell, who was a member of the Washington chapter of the group. It works well in a bigger group of older players who are well versed in movies, books, plays, and songs. A high IQ is optional.

NUMBER OF PLAYERS	2 to 12
AGE	13 and up
YOU WILL NEED	Good general knowledge of movie, song, play, and book titles
PLAYING TIME	10 minutes per round

OBJECT OF THE GAME
To create a chain of associated titles. The more creative and lateral the association, the better the game.

HOW TO PLAY
Players form a circle with the 'Carnelli Master' standing in the centre. The Master points to one of the players and says a title of a book, movie, or song: say, *Romeo and Juliet*. That player must think of an associated title: say, *Macbeth*. In that example, the titles are similar in that they share an author. Alternatively, they may share a producer, mutual star, or related words. The next player to their left must think of another associated title: remembering

that they recently heard about the Shakespeare play series *War of the Roses*, they might state this. The next player happens to know that Cate Blanchett starred in that production as Richard II, and so (thinking laterally), they might state the title of a movie that she has been in (*Elizabeth*, for example). And on it goes.

You can see how this game could get really interesting and creative, particularly for those with extensive general knowledge of, and a good memory for, titles. Puns such as *Tequila Sunrise* and *To Kill a Mockingbird* (pronounced Te-quil-a Mockingbird) are allowed, and are even encouraged by hammed-up groans from the audience.

Any player can challenge a title. If someone challenges successfully, the player who made the association steps out. If the challenge is not successful, the challenger has to step out. The Carnelli Master has great control over what is allowed: all his decisions are final, no matter how capricious.

The Carnelli Master also keeps a time limit (say, 30 seconds) for each title: if players can't think of one in the designated time or declare a title that isn't allowed, they must step out. The last remaining player is the winner.

You can see how raucous this game could get — definitely a good one for after dinner. Perhaps this one even deserves a Carnelli night on its own, with a few like-minded friends.

IN THE PARLOUR WITH JUNE

Dr June Factor is a well-known writer and scholar in the field of children's culture and folklore. She is a senior research fellow at the Australian Centre, University of Melbourne.

In the 1970s, when she was teaching at the Institute of Childhood Development in Melbourne, she sent her student teachers out on assignment to record the games and rhymes that they saw children playing on the playground. Her aim was to remind them of their own childhood, so that they could better connect with children.

Nearly 40 years later, this pioneering work forms part of a collection of more than 10,000 children's games, rhymes, riddles, jokes, superstitions, and other kinds of children's folklore, which is held at the Australian Children's Folklore Collection at the Melbourne Museum.

Some of these have been recorded in her popular children's books *Far Out, Brussel Sprout!*, *Real Keen, Baked Bean!*, *All Right, Vegemite!*, *Roll Over, Pavlova!*, *Unreal, Banana Peel!*, and *Okey Dokey, Karaoke!*

We spent an afternoon with June in her parlour, a sun-filled room with a big table, where the topic of children's play could be explored with expansive gestures. This is what June had to say:

Children rarely write anything down that they say; playthings are thrown out: people don't keep Jacks, they don't keep marbles. And so, when my student teachers brought back the games, the rhymes, the riddles, the sayings, I knew I had to keep them. That's how I began. It's a bit like being bitten by the malarial mosquito: once it's in the bloodstream, you can't get rid of it.

I tell you, it drives me to drink how little play is understood, and how vastly it is ignored. Play is absolutely at the core of childhood. Children have to be very ill in body or mind not to play. Even children in difficult and dangerous circumstances still play.

Play is a way in which children make sense of the world. It is the intermediary space between the outside world, the world of gravity, the world of tables and chairs, the world of all-powerful parents; and the inner world, the world of dream and fantasy and nightmare, thought and feeling. It is like a magic arena where kids can try things out.

Some people have amazing recollections of their childhood games, others not. But everyone has once been a child, and everyone has played. Most play among children is initiated by them, and is often part of an ancient tradition of playlore, inherited from previous generations of children and adapted to suit current circumstances.

There are different types of games. With card games, for example, adults have a role to play in passing down knowledge. These sorts of games, more traditionally, come from adults to children. They become part of the net that holds the family together, and may form some of the best memories that the children will have of family life — so long as the games don't turn into lectures. To use a rather overused term, parents ought to be facilitators, rather than instructors. They provide the material, they show children how it can be done, and they join in; but they should resist being the boss.

Games can't always be learnt all at once, and we can't always be good at them. You are not playing for the game, you are playing for the children. If it is too intense, or too difficult, or too upsetting, then drop it!

Parents need to know that they are part of a chain, a chain that probably stretches to the beginnings of humanity. They are only a link in that chain; they are not the masters of it. They never created it. They are simply passing on play traditions to children. The major links in the chain are children themselves. The kids are the tradition-bearers.

GAMES WITH STORIES

I like a good story well told. That is the reason
I am sometimes forced to tell them myself.
— Mark Twain

You don't have to be Mark Twain to tell a good story. Children tend to be natural storytellers, when their imaginations are allowed to run riot. Sometimes, the shyest child can come up with the most surprising oratory; and the most serious, with the wackiest speech.

The following games are based on telling a story big and small, long and tall; from those that depend on the communal efforts of the group (Endless Story) to those that require you to use your best powers of description (the Colander Game). And then, there are those that reward you for talking on one topic without repetition, deviation, or hesitation (After-Dinner Speeches). Let's see you talk your way out of that one.

ENDLESS STORY

This is great for little imaginations: the smaller the player, the more novel and fantastic the story. This works just as well around the dinner table as it does around the campfire, and is a great spontaneous game for a bit of a laugh.

NUMBER OF PLAYERS	3 or more (the bigger the group, the better)
AGE	4 and up
YOU WILL NEED	A good imagination and the ability to think on your feet
PLAYING TIME	10 minutes per story

OBJECT OF THE GAME
To tell a good, or a tall, story without hesitating.

HOW TO PLAY

The participants sit in a circle, and one of them starts a story about anything at all. He may continue for a couple of sentences. Without finishing the story, he touches the person on his right, who must continue the narrative, even in the middle of a sentence. This continues until the chain reaches the person who started it, who must bring it to a successful end. If someone goes on too long, they may need a bit of gentle prodding to move it along.

There are no winners or losers in the game: the point is to come up with the most interesting or funniest story that you can.

VARIATION

Players sit in a circle, and one person starts a story with a word. The person to their right continues with another word, and so on, until they have come up with a very ridiculous communal sentence, or even a story, if you keep it going around long enough.

INTERVIEWS

This is a game that we thought up while on holidays, after reading a column in a newspaper in which standard questions are asked of various well-known people. We used some of these questions to 'interview' our own family, with hysterical and revealing results.

NUMBER OF PLAYERS	2 or more
AGE	6 and up
YOU WILL NEED	Some pre-designed questions to ask players
PLAYING TIME	10 to 15 minutes

OBJECT OF THE GAME

To find out as many interesting things as you can about players by interviewing them.

HOW TO PLAY

One person interviews other players. We have included a list of questions, but budding reporters will have fun making up any questions they like. It is best to put a cap on the number of questions (say, ten) so that every player has a chance to be interviewed: keeping it pacey ensures that players answer honestly and spontaneously.

1. What is your earliest memory?
2. What was your most embarrassing moment?
3. What was your happiest moment?
4. If you could time-travel, where would you go to?
5. When was the last time you drank too much? (a very comical question to ask a six-year-old!)
6. When was the last time you lied?
7. What is your favourite book?
8. What do you consider your best quality?
9. What skill should you have learnt?
10. If you could do anything, what would it be?

Why not record the answers, and play the game again in a year's time to see what's changed?

AFTER-DINNER SPEECHES

This is a very funny game that was popular in Victorian times.

NUMBER OF PLAYERS	2 to 12
AGE	7 and up
YOU WILL NEED	A watch or clock with a second hand, paper and pen, and a container of some sort
PLAYING TIME	5 to 10 minutes per round

OBJECT OF THE GAME

To speak continuously about a topic without hesitation, deviation, or repetition for one minute.

HOW TO PLAY

Everyone thinks of a topic for a one-minute speech. It could be anything from the etiquette of farting (very popular with little boys) to olives (one of our kids' suggestions). Each player writes their topic on a piece of paper, folds that paper, and puts it into a container. If there are only two of you, commit the subject to memory. In the case of bigger groups, someone will need to be a designated host, to keep time and settle disputes.

The host pulls a slip of paper from the container and reads out the topic. The first player needs to speak for up to one minute on that topic, without repetition, hesitation, or deviation.

If the speaker stumbles, if they waffle on aimlessly, or if they repeat themselves, the host stops the watch and the speaker is challenged. Words in the title of the topic and words such as 'and' and 'but' are allowed to be used repetitively.

Any player who makes a correct challenge against the speaker is awarded one point and the chance to take over the speech for the remaining minute. The entertaining bit of this game is in deciding what is deemed a 'correct' challenge. Any player who challenges the speaker must convince the host (who has the final say) that the speaker repeated a word, that they deviated from the topic, or that they stumbled.

If a challenge is deemed incorrect, the speaker earns one point and continues the speech. Anyone who is speaking at the end of one minute also scores a point. If someone speaks for a whole minute without being challenged, they earn a bonus point. This is much harder than it sounds; it seems to be human nature to waffle.

You will need a very firm settler of disputes, as the challenges can get riotous. The speaker is allowed to try to justify their waffle (sometimes leading to more waffle); but, at the end of day, the dispute needs to be settled by the host.

Played well, this is a very entertaining game, both in seeing how creative the speaker can be and in seeing how entertaining and amusing the rationale for the interruptions can be.

VARIATION

For younger players, who may not really appreciate the interruptions in this game and the finer points around the rules, a simpler version can be played. As above, each player can speak on a chosen topic for one minute, or even 30 seconds, in the case of quite young players. The person who speaks for the longest without hesitation, deviation, or repetition wins that round. The person who wins the most rounds overall is declared the winner.

DID YOU KNOW?

This game was popularised by the BBC with its *Just a Minute* radio program, in which chairman Nicholas Parsons tries to keep control over a roll call of celebrity contenders who talk on a subject for 60 seconds without hesitation, repetition, or deviation.

The program was created by the late Ian Messiter, who remembered being given the horrible task of repeating, without hesitation or deviation, what one of his school masters had been saying during a minute in which he had been staring out the window. He failed dismally. It is said that some sort of corporal punishment ensued.

Initially, BBC producers were sceptical about whether the series would run for more than six programs. Thirty-five years later, the show attracts two million listeners.

IT COULD BE WORSE

It's frightening how funny this game can be, considering you have to think of the most catastrophic scenario that you can.

NUMBER OF PLAYERS	2 or more
AGES	7 and up
YOU WILL NEED	To catastrophise well
PLAYING TIME	5 minutes per round

OBJECT OF THE GAME
To think of the worst thing you can.

HOW TO PLAY
Players sit in a circle. The starting player describes a fairly unassuming event; for example, 'I was late for school this morning.' The second player tries to top that by proposing how the event could have been worse; for example, 'It could be worse: you could have tripped on a log on the way to school.' Then, the next player proposes something worse again; for example, 'It could be worse: you could have hurt your head and been taken to hospital.' And so on, until the worst-case scenario has been thought of, in which case another innocuous event is described and the game starts over. It fast becomes apparent when playing this game that some people are great catastrophists.

THE COLANDER GAME

This game is really a verbal version of Charades, good for when you are not in the mood to get up out of your chair. It relies on clear and concise verbal descriptions from players, so it exercises spoken skills very well.

NUMBER OF PLAYERS	2 or more
AGE	8 and up
YOU WILL NEED	A few scraps of paper, a container (or colander, as the name suggests), and a stopwatch or a watch with a second hand
PLAYING TIME	15 to 20 minutes

OBJECT OF THE GAME

To correctly guess the most names within one minute from the verbal descriptions provided.

HOW TO PLAY

Each player tears a piece of paper into ten small pieces and writes the name of a person on each piece. That person can be a fictional character, a celebrity, or someone known to everyone in the group. The papers are then folded and placed in the container.

To start, one player takes a piece of paper from the container. They must try to describe the person named on the paper to the person to their left. They can do anything but say the name on the paper (impressions and 'sounds like' clues are allowed). For example: 'He is the prime minister of Australia, he wears glasses, he goes to church …'

They continue doing this for one minute, describing as many names as they can get through, with the other player all the while calling out their guesses. The guesser keeps the papers that they have guessed correctly as a record of their score.

When one minute is up, the person who was guessing takes the colander, and play continues with the person to their left until there are no more papers left in the container or the company tires. The person with the most bits of paper at the end wins.

CONVERSATIONS

Also known as ABC, this is a great game that requires you to converse on a particular topic by starting each sentence with consecutive letters of the alphabet. The beauty of this game is that you can add layers of difficulty, and an element of competition, by introducing timing.

NUMBER OF PLAYERS	3 to 13
AGE	9 and up
YOU WILL NEED	The ability to think quickly
PLAYING TIME	10 to 15 minutes

OBJECT OF THE GAME
To keep a topic of conversation going by using sentences that begin with consecutive letters of the alphabet.

HOW TO PLAY
The first player must start a conversation with a sentence that begins with a word starting with any letter of the alphabet. The next player continues, with a sentence that begins with a word starting with the next letter of the alphabet. Each person follows the conversation through the alphabet, ending back with the letter with which they started. For younger players, the conversation can be free-flowing, but for older players it may be an extra challenge to choose and stick to one topic. For example, if a chosen topic is skating:

John: 'Hey, let's go skating today.'
Mary: 'I think skating is a great idea.'
Chris: 'Just thinking about skating makes me fall over.'
John: 'Kath will be there; she can show you how to do it.'
Mary: 'Lucky for you, Chris!'
Chris: 'Maybe we should go, then.'

Whoever hesitates for too long or can't think of anything to say drops out, until there is only one person standing and, of course, they are the winner.

VARIATION

This version is called Alphabet Minute. If you have a bigger group, split up into teams and see how many letters each team can get through in 60 seconds. The group that (correctly) gets through the most letters wins.

GAMES TO CONFUSE AND CONFOUND

According to the *Macquarie Dictionary*, one of the archaic meanings of 'confound' is 'to defeat or overthrow; bring to ruin or naught'. Well, we certainly don't hope to bring you to ruin, but some of these games are sure to get your brain in a bit of a twist. Perhaps they should come with a warning: the following games will perplex, bewilder, and even befuddle. Proceed with caution.

Our favourites include Buzz and the maddening Fizz Buzz, during which you can almost feel the cogs going around in your brain. Then, there's the addictive Slap, Clap, Click, Speak, not to mention the very cheeky Taboo. Oh, you are going to have so much fun getting confused.

CHINESE WHISPERS

Also known as Telephone, Gossip, Arab Phone, Russian Scandal, and *Stille Post* (Silent Post), this game is often referred to by adults as a caution against the dangers of rumour or gossip. Perhaps when you have played the game a couple of times, you can ask children if there are any lessons to be learnt from it. It is most successful if played in a big group.

NUMBER OF PLAYERS	4 or more (the more the better)
AGE	5 and up
YOU WILL NEED	Careful listening skills
PLAYING TIME	5 minutes

OBJECT OF THE GAME
There is no winner: the entertainment comes from comparing the original and final messages.

HOW TO PLAY

Form a circle. One player whispers some little incident into the ear of his neighbour — perhaps a rumour, or even a funny joke. For younger players, this could be a single word. The recipient of the news then whispers it to the next player, and so on, around the circle, till the 'whisper' comes back to the original whisperer. If the circle is only made of a few players, it may go around a few times before it stops. The whisper is then repeated aloud and compared to the original. Is it the same or altogether different?

Usually, the whisper differs significantly, and amusingly, from its original wording.

TABOO

What does the word 'taboo' mean, and what does it have to do with explorer Captain James Cook? Read on and you'll find out. This game is bound to get your brain in a twist.

NUMBER OF PLAYERS	2 to 12
AGE	6 and up
YOU WILL NEED	An ability to stay alert and not lapse into mental laziness
PLAYING TIME	5 minutes per round

OBJECT OF THE GAME

To replace a selected word with the word 'taboo'.

HOW TO PLAY

All players agree on a small word, such as 'and', 'the', 'it' or 'on', to be replaced by the word 'taboo'.

One player is then chosen to ask the questions. This player puts questions to all the other players about absolutely anything, in order to make them use the taboo word. He may interrupt them mid-sentence with another question, in order to force them to accidentally use the taboo word. For example, if the taboo word is 'and':

Dolores: 'What did you have for breakfast this morning?'
Emmanuel: 'I had toast, bacon taboo eggs.'
Dolores: 'Did you have anything else with them?'
Emmanuel: 'Yes, I had juice taboo a sweet afterwards, too!'

Anyone who uses the taboo word immediately drops out of the round, as does anyone who hesitates too long in giving their answer. The last player left is the winner. The faster the game gets, the harder it is to remember not to use the taboo word. If there are only two players, it may help if each person has three chances, which helps with continuity.

DID YOU KNOW?

The English explorer Captain James Cook, visiting Tonga in 1773 and 1777, referred to this group of islands as 'the Friendly Islands', such a warm welcome did he get there. But he also noted the strict prohibitions that islanders observed. He wrote in his journal in 1777: 'Not one of them would sit down, or eat a bit of any thing … On expressing my surprise at this, they were all taboo … [which,] in general, signifies that a thing is forbidden …'

From its origins in Polynesia, the word 'taboo' has travelled as widely as Cook himself, and is now used throughout the English-speaking world.

VARIATION

For those who have mastered this version of Taboo, try challenging your brains further by choosing one letter of the alphabet as a taboo letter. The idea is that every word using that letter is taboo. Good luck!

AND FOR A BIT OF A LAUGH …

One of our kids asked: 'Could you use another word instead of "taboo"? Like "Chihuahua"? That's a breed of dog,' she patiently explained. Then, she went on to give an example, replacing the word 'and' with 'Chihuahua':

'What did you have for breakfast?'

'I had toast, Chihuahua milk, Chihuahua a piece of fruit.'

It made us all laugh. Why not use other funny words to replace the word 'taboo'?

SLAP, CLAP, CLICK, SPEAK

Also known as Names of …, this is a group clapping game that requires a certain amount of hand and brain coordination, as well as good concentration. It takes a little bit of practice and skill, but is great fun, and is likely to lead to quite a bit of laughter, especially in a big group.

NUMBER OF PLAYERS	3 or more (the more the better)
AGE	8 and up
YOU WILL NEED	Rhythm and concentration
PLAYING TIME	5 to 10 minutes

OBJECT OF THE GAME

Not to miss the beat.

HOW TO PLAY

Players sit in a circle with their legs crossed. The more players you have, the better. One person is picked to be the leader and starts by getting the rhythm going: slap on thighs, a clap, and two snaps of the fingers (first with the right hand, then with the left). So, the rhythm sounds like this: slap, clap, snap, snap. When everyone has picked up the same rhythm, the leader thinks of a category. Players can speak, one at a time, in turn, on the rhythmic snap of the fingers.

The play goes like this:

Sophie: Slap, clap … then, on the snap, snap: 'Names of …'
Joshua: Slap, clap … then, on the snap, snap: 'Ani-mals.'
Ahmed: Slap, clap … then, on the snap, snap: 'Don-keys.'
Sophie: Slap, clap … then, on the snap, snap: 'Rhino-ceros.'
Joshua: Slap, clap … then, on the snap, snap: 'Jag-uars.'

It doesn't matter how many syllables are in the word, so long as they are said in time with the beat. The same word cannot be repeated twice.

When a player makes a mistake, either by saying a word out of rhythm, missing a beat, not saying something quickly enough, or repeating a word, they are out. The next person in line picks up the rhythm again. Play continues until only one player remains. If the momentum lags, one person should take the initiative and make it harder by suddenly changing the category, making the rhythm faster, or adding another action to the game, such as winking after the word.

Happy slap, clap, snap, snapping!

BUZZ

This very 'more-ish' game is a great way for younger players to practise counting and for middle-school children to learn multiples of seven. Not only is it great for mathematical learning, it's also a fantastic concentration game. It's amazing how hard it is to substitute a number with a word, and how lazy one's brain gets when on automatic pilot.

NUMBER OF PLAYERS	2 to 12
AGE	8 and up (simple version)
YOU WILL NEED	Your wits about you
PLAYING TIME	5 minutes per round

OBJECT OF THE GAME

To say 'buzz' every time you come to a number with seven in it, or any multiple of seven, in the count to one hundred.

HOW TO PLAY

The first player says 'one', the next 'two', the next 'three', and so on, until seven is reached. Instead of saying 'seven', the player whose turn it is must say 'buzz'. This continues every time they come to a number that has a seven in it, and until they come to one hundred. At 77, a player must say 'buzz-buzz'.

At every multiple of seven — 14, 21, 28, 35, 42, etc. — the word 'buzz' must also be substituted. Sound confusing? That's the aim of this game.

Any player who fails to 'buzz' at the appropriate time, or hesitates too long, is out of the game. The last player remaining is the winner.

VARIATIONS

For younger players, the game can be played by only replacing numbers containing the digit seven (for example, saying 'buzz' at seven, 17, 27, etc.). Alternatively, it may help to choose an easier number to multiply, such as five.

FIZZ AND FIZZ-BUZZ

NUMBER OF PLAYERS	2 to 12
AGE	10 and up
YOU WILL NEED	Even more wits about you
PLAYING TIME	5 to 10 minutes per round

OBJECT OF THE GAME

To say 'fizz', 'buzz', and 'fizz-buzz' at the right times, in the count to one hundred.

HOW TO PLAY

Fizz is played in the same way as Buzz, but another number is substituted: say, three. Every time a player comes to the number three or a multiple of it, they substitute the word 'fizz'.

Once you've mastered that, try the very complicated Fizz-Buzz. The premise here is that you say 'buzz' whenever you come to either the number seven or multiples of seven, and 'fizz' whenever you come to the number three or multiples of three. For example: one, two, fizz, four, five, fizz, buzz, eight, fizz, ten, 11, fizz, fizz, buzz, fizz, 16, buzz, fizz, 19, 20, fizz-buzz (because 21 is both a multiple of three and seven), 22, fizz, fizz, 25, etc.

THANK YOU, THANK YOU!

We would like to acknowledge the contribution of the following people to making this book:

Margot Rosenbloom, for the inspiration and all her input and ideas.

Henry Rosenbloom, publisher at Scribe, for signing us up.

Jacinta di Mase, for representing us and our book.

Nicola Redhouse, for the fantastic editing job, and Ian See for meticulous proof-reading.

Miriam Rosenbloom and Dave Altheim, for the great design, and Joe McLaren, for the playful illustrations.

Ross and Damian at the Macelleria Salumeria Italiana, Australian–Continental Butcher in North Carlton, for collecting our knucklebones.

Bernie DeKoven, for giving us the gift of his time and immense wisdom about fun and games.

June Factor, for sharing her passion and enthusiasm about children's play.

George Perry, for sharing with us stories of his childhood games.

The ladies from the Leicestershire lawn-bowls club, for sharing the Victorian parlour games they learnt from their grandmothers.

Jono Burns, for a whole heap of wonderful dramatic games.

The marvellous modern families who tested games for us and gave us their feedback: the Allisons, the Cachias, the Cross-Joneses, the Cuskelly-Fitzgeralds, the di Mases, the Harvey-O'Connors, the LayClarks, the Lightfoot-Trifilettis, the Nallaratnams, the Petrases, the Skog-Whytes; and Adelle Mansour, Josephine Mifsud, Katerina Tzikas, and Monica Marshall.

To the rest of our family and friends, too numerous to name, for offering us their games, their playful memories, and their enthusiasm for the project.

And finally to our very own modern families — George, Dolores, and Emmanuel; and James, Marlon, and Llewellyn — we thank you from the bottom of our hearts for participating in the year-long games marathon, and for helping to make it such a fun journey.

Thank you, thank you!!

INDEX

PENGUIN HISTORY

THE ENGLISH YEAR
STEVE ROUD

This enthralling book will take you, month-by-month, day-by-day, through all the festivities of English life. From national celebrations such as New Year's Eve to regional customs such as the Padstow Hobby Horse procession, cheese rolling in Gloucestershire and Easter Monday bottle kicking in Leeds, it explains how they originated, what they mean and when they occur.

A fascinating guide to the richness of our heritage and the sometimes eccentric nature of life in England, *The English Year* offers a unique chronological view of our social customs and attitudes.

'The book is a delight, a fund of information' *The Times*

PARTICULAR BOOKS

WHY IS Q ALWAYS FOLLOWED BY U?
MICHAEL QUINION

Long-time word-detective and bestselling author of *Port Out, Starboard Home*, Michael Quinion brings us the answers to nearly two hundred of the most intriguing questions he's been asked about language over the years. Sent to him by enquiring readers from all around the globe, Michael's answers about the meanings and histories behind the quirky phrases, slang and language that we all use are set to delight, amuse and enlighten even the most hardened word-obsessive.

• Did you know that 'Blighty' comes from an ancient Arabic word?

• Or that Liberace cried his way to the bank so many times people think he came up with the phrase?

• That 'cloud nine' started out as 'cloud seven' in the speakeasies of '30s America?

• And that the first person to have their thunder stolen was a dismal playwright from Drury Lane?

Why is Q Always Followed By U? is full of surprising discoveries, entertaining quotations and memorable information. Michael Quinion will help you discover the truth that lies behind the *cock-and-bull* stories and make sure you're always linguistically *on the ball*.

'Quinion brilliantly tackles the riddles of so many of the sayings we've long puzzled over: he's authoritative, quirky, and always entertaining' Susie Dent

PARTICULAR BOOKS

WHAT CAESAR DID FOR MY SALAD:
NOT TO MENTION THE EARL'S SANDWICH, PAVLOVA'S MERINGUE
AND OTHER CURIOUS STORIES BEHIND OUR FAVOURITE FOOD
ALBERT JACK

Did you know that the Cornish pasty was invented to protect tin miners from
arsenic poisoning?

What biscuit is named after an Italian revolutionary or that the word 'salary' comes
from Roman soldiers being paid their wages in salt?

Where does cheese-rolling come from or hot-cross buns? Is the 'french fry' a
conspiracy to steal the chip from the British?

And when it comes to salad, did you know the Ancient Egyptians saw lettuce as a
potent aphrodisiac . . .

We have become so obsessed with checking ingredients and calorie counting that
we've lost sight of the bizarre stories behind our favourite dishes and where they
come from (not to mention their unusual creators). What *Caesar Did For My Salad*
is crammed full of fascinating insights, characters and incidents; this hilarious
book has enough stories to entertain a hundred dinner parties.

PENGUIN HUMOUR

SHAGGY DOGS & BLACK SHEEP
ALBERT JACK

The English language is crammed with colourful phrases and sayings that we use without thinking every day. It's only when we're asked who *smart Alec* or *Holy Moly* were, where feeling *in the pink* or *once in a blue moon* come from that we realize that there's far more to English than we might have thought.

Luckily enough, we have Albert Jack, who has explored the origins of hundreds of phrases from around the world. The fascinating stories he has uncovered come from the rich traditions of the navy, army and law to confidence tricksters and highwaymen, from the practices of ancient civilizations to Music Hall and pubs.

Shaggy Dogs and Black Sheep is a compulsively readable, highly enlightening look at the phrases we use all the time but rarely consider. From the skin of your teeth to the graveyard shift – you'll never speak (or even think) English in the same way again.

'Just "the bees knees" . . . you'll never think of English in the same way again' *Irish Times*

PENGUIN COOKERY

MASTERING THE ART OF FRENCH COOKING: VOLUME 1
JULIA CHILD, LOUISETTE BERTHOLLE AND SIMONE BECK

The legendary cookbook that inspired *Julie and Julia*.

'This isn't just any cookery book. It is *Mastering the Art of French Cooking*, first published in 1961, and it's a book that is a statement, not of culinary intent, but of aspiration, a commitment to a certain sort of good life, a certain sort of world-view; a votive object implying taste and appetite and a little *je ne sais quoi*. Julia Child was like Amelia Earhart, or Eleanor Roosevelt: she was a hero who'd gone out there and made a difference. Her books are a triumph, and also a trophy'
AA Gill, *The Times*

'The most instructive book on fine French cooking written in the English language'
Elizabeth David

'This book fundamentally altered the way a basic human activity was perceived and pursued' A. O. Scott, *The New York Times*

'Has been described as being the best book about French cooking in English ... I agree' Ambrose Heath, *Guardian*

He just wanted a decent book to read ...

Not too much to ask, is it? It was in 1935 when Allen Lane, Managing Director of Bodley Head Publishers, stood on a platform at Exeter railway station looking for something good to read on his journey back to London. His choice was limited to popular magazines and poor-quality paperbacks – the same choice faced every day by the vast majority of readers, few of whom could afford hardbacks. Lane's disappointment and subsequent anger at the range of books generally available led him to found a company – and change the world.

'We believed in the existence in this country of a vast reading public for intelligent books at a low price, and staked everything on it'
Sir Allen Lane, 1902–1970, founder of Penguin Books

The quality paperback had arrived – and not just in bookshops. Lane was adamant that his Penguins should appear in chain stores and tobacconists, and should cost no more than a packet of cigarettes.

Reading habits (and cigarette prices) have changed since 1935, but Penguin still believes in publishing the best books for everybody to enjoy. We still believe that good design costs no more than bad design, and we still believe that quality books published passionately and responsibly make the world a better place.

So wherever you see the little bird – whether it's on a piece of prize-winning literary fiction or a celebrity autobiography, political tour de force or historical masterpiece, a serial-killer thriller, reference book, world classic or a piece of pure escapism – you can bet that it represents the very best that the genre has to offer.

Whatever you like to read – trust Penguin.